T0323803

SURVIVING THE COLLEGE APPLICATION PROCESS

The college admissions landscape and the steps to apply can be overwhelming and confusing! This mini guide is a quick resource highlighting key components to consider in the effort to decode and demystify the college application process for the college-bound student and their family.

Covering topics such as essential application components, standardizing testing, personal statements, and financial aid, *Surviving the College Application Process* is your secret weapon for navigating the college research, planning, and selection process.

Light-hearted and accessible, this book can be read from cover to cover or referenced as needed by college-bound students, their families, school counselors, and anyone interested in post-secondary education.

Jennifer Romano is a high school counselor with over 18 years of experience helping students achieve academic, social, and personal success through their unique lens as they navigate post-secondary goals.

SURVIVING THE COLLEGE APPLICATION PROCESS

A POCKET RESEARCH AND PLANNING GUIDE FOR STUDENTS

Jennifer Romano

NEW YORK AND LONDON

Designed cover image: © Getty Images

First published 2024
by Routledge
605 Third Avenue, New York, NY 10158

and by Routledge
4 Park Square, Milton Park, Abingdon, Oxon, OX14 4RN

Routledge is an imprint of the Taylor & Francis Group, an informa business

© 2024 Jennifer Romano

Library of Congress Cataloging-in-Publication Data
Names: Romano, Jennifer, author.
Title: Surviving the college application process : a pocket research and planning guide for students / Jennifer Romano.
Description: New York, NY : Routledge, 2024. | Includes bibliographical references. |
Identifiers: LCCN 2023027303 (print) | LCCN 2023027304 (ebook) | ISBN 9781032459417 (paperback) | ISBN 9781003380948 (ebook)
Subjects: LCSH: Universities and colleges—United States—Admission. | College choice—United States.
Classification: LCC LB2351.2 .R66 2024 (print) | LCC LB2351.2 (ebook) | DDC 378.1/61—dc23/eng/20230810
LC record available at https://lccn.loc.gov/2023027303
LC ebook record available at https://lccn.loc.gov/2023027304

ISBN: 978-1-032-45941-7 (pbk)
ISBN: 978-1-003-38094-8 (ebk)

DOI: 10.4324/9781003380948

Typeset in Bembo
by Apex CoVantage, LLC

CONTENTS

Part 5
After acceptance **89**

INTRODUCTION

First, I take no credit for knowing it all, or a lot, for the manner of speaking "college". For as soon as anyone feels on top their game, the rules change, and the drafting paper comes out—we're back to the drawing board.

I think of the college planning, research, and the application process as a fine art. Students and families who undergo these processes mostly identify in unique and yet some parallel and intersecting ways with others. There are three known truths to the overall 'college process'—one, it is a process—an unveiling and a journey not to be taken lightly by the traveler, otherwise known as the college-bound student. It must be respected. It must not be rushed. Students, be prepared to be transformed. Second, and perhaps more important than the first, there is a college for everyone: a new home, a new experience, a new beginning. Thirdly, and even more important than the first two—what you've all been waiting for—the secrets to getting in. Well, I hate to break it to you, but there are no secret formulas, folks, but there are tools and factors that we can use to gauge a student's targeted likelihood for admission.

As a school counselor, I would be remiss if I did not get on my soapbox about mental health, perspective, and balance among all things 'life'. College, and the pursuit thereof, does not matter if we do not care for ourselves, mind our minds, and balance the many facets and demands within our lives. If students have taken more of a permanent residence in their bedrooms swallowed up by homework, apps, and SAT® and ACT® prep, finding little sleep and no time for interaction among friends and with family, then we must reevaluate our goals and reposition our scale. Imbalance creates insecurity, ill-preparedness, and feelings of ineptitude. Balance creates perspective, pause, and preparedness.

"SAT, is a registered trademark of the College Board and the National Merit Scholarship Corporation."
"ACT® is a trademark registered by ACT, Inc., which is not affiliated with, and does not endorse, this product. www.act.org."

PART 1

WHERE TO APPLY?

COLLEGE-BOUND FOR EVERYONE?

My experience has afforded me the awareness that while there is a college out there for everyone—a right-size-fits-all model—not everyone wants to attend college, and maybe not everyone *should* attend college. Let me shout it to the hilltops—this is okay! Many students find success in school-to-career opportunities; just the same find success in attending a two-year community college from which some may then transfer to a four-year institution.

As if deciding whether to attend college was difficult enough, the decision on *where to attend* and at which *type* of institution can be even more daunting. There are close to 5,000 two- and four-year colleges in the United States alone. Sifting through them can seem overwhelming, but there are ample resources to help students do so.

UTILIZING SOFTWARE PROGRAMS FOR COLLEGE RESEARCH

For one, high school juniors should be reaching out to their assigned school counselor to identify their college planning and research computer programs. Naviance® by PowerSchool® and Scoir® are two very popular software programs that pair up with high school data and are designed so that students can explore colleges, career pathways, and conduct college readiness assessments. Through Naviance's SuperMatch® search tool, for example, and the College Board BigFuture®, a web-based app, students not only identify colleges that meet their criteria and interests through what I like to call a "fit" category, but they can also rank the likelihood of acceptance

DOI: 10.4324/9781003380948-2

through tools such as "how do I compare" or "how do I rate" features found within each platform.

ASSESSING YOUR PREFERENCES

It is important to assess students' innate abilities to self-navigate independent living, handle time management, as well as assess internal drive and motivation to succeed when thinking about college. It is equally important to acknowledge a student's level of maturity and literacy of all things "life" from all aspects: social, emotional, academic, interpersonal, conflict resolution, and financial, just to name a few.

Questions you should ask yourself

Students, ask yourself the following: Do you see yourself living on a college campus close to home where you could feasibly travel home on a weekend or during the week if needed? Do you envision living on campus where travel home would be sporadic and only on major holidays either by car, train, or even plane? Is your ideal campus a large (>15,000 students), medium (6,000–15,000 students), or small campus (<5000 students)?

Do you prefer lecture-type classes with upwards of 300 students? Or would you prefer more intimate discussions in a classroom of 10–30 students? Location, size, and type of environment matter. Deep South or east coast?

Do you prefer a college in the city, or near a major city that may offer an open and busy city with street access and public transportation? Or do you prefer colleges with a town or suburban feel, where a campus may feel more closed and fully self-sustaining (ATM or bank, laundromat, dry cleaner, and fast-food and other restaurants located on the campus)?

FIT GOES BOTH WAYS

No matter the type of institution one attends, college is an investment across all playing fields: academic, social, emotional, financial, and personal. Students must prepare themselves to engage in exciting but unfamiliar territories. Just where a student is in his, her, or their journey will look different for everyone. The process of finding a future "home" should not be taken lightly.

Learning about self and *how* and *why* one is motivated and geared towards acquiring new knowledge is extremely constructive in determining *place* of learning and *style* of learning environment. Just as it is important for a student to understand *self* in relation to *other* (other meaning the campus, climate, and culture of a campus, inclusive of all things education and academic), it is equally important for campuses and institutions to acquire knowledge of the candidate for their benefit and well-being. In short, fit goes both ways. I would like to borrow from University of Pennsylvania's former Dean of Admissions and, most recently, Senior Associate Director of College Counseling at a charter school in Philadelphia, Eric Furda's, originated phraseology—a framework consisting of five Is and four Cs which delineates key buzzwords—super scoring components that are inextricably embedded (or should be) into one's college exploratory, application, final decision, and commitment stages of the overall college application process. The buzzwords now appear in a written work co-authored with himself and Jacques Steinberg. The framework is an assignment of one's take on self-assessment in the eyes of college review committees, but also on how the self is idealized by the applicant. Deciding and reviewing a college through this scaffolding can only better allow a more perfect two-way *fit* in the eyes of the candidate. How one envisions themselves on campus and through various means he/she/they are exposed to learning and held in interest to these teachings through inspiration and captivation is key. Students must also look at the inner culture and climate of a campus, what activities or innovations define the campus, where a candidate wants to end their journey, and in what capacity and through which processes while also asking what *conclusion or outcome* one wants.

The five "I"s refer to the *student applicant as "self."* What motivates the student, *how* does one like to learn, *what* makes one *tick*, and *where* does one's interests fall? Essentially, what makes up the student? And, better yet, what type of institution will speak to them? The four "C"s refer to elements on a student's *wish list* that define the campus such as culture, community, and curriculum. Together, along with some great insight on behalf of the student, one begins to define *fit* and the unique parameters of this type of fit appropriate for the individual student. For greater reference and an expansive list and description, please source Eric Furda and Jacques Steinberg (2020).

REFERENCE

Eric Furda and Jacques Steinberg. *The College Conversation: A Practical Companion for Parents to Guide Their Children Along the Path to High Education.* New York: Penguin Random House, 2020.

 ## KEY TAKEAWAYS

There are various apps and software platforms that can help guide students in the college research process.

College is an investment from all angles: social, emotional, and financial.

Understanding yourself as a student-learner, dorm mate and room-mate, academic and inter-personable being—all things on how to navigate life—is a huge first step in researching colleges and knowing which ones are a good fit.

Fit goes both ways.

TRENDS OF A FOREVER-CHANGING COLLEGE LANDSCAPE

Undeniably, the COVID-19 pandemic, mid and post, has greatly impacted the college process for high school students and the college experience for matriculated students from angles such as research, planning, reviewing, visiting, applying, attending, and navigating campus, and, students, you know how COVID has impacted you directly. Colleges and universities have responded to safety measures by implementing structural changes in their organization to create safer living and learning conditions for students. Many changes appear through the development of vaccine protocols, masking determinations, close contact protocols, and, in some cases, low to restricted visitation caps. Some COVID-related adaptations have resulted in permanent changes within the admissions and applicant review processes primarily due to the lack of college admissions testing availability considering test center shutdowns across the globe. This leads the charge for close to 1,000 colleges entering the test-optional arena, thereby changing college admissions review processes, in some cases, for good. Many colleges have taken permanent residency on the test-optional list, which has encouraged those formerly less likely to apply to now push forward, full throttle. The once considered SAT®/ACT® score data is no longer a barrier for many otherwise average, but unique, applicants whose application may have been less attractive with the submission of scores. Some would graciously offer that the admissions game has become fairer. One can also agree that, with this relaxation of score determinants, many fresh, new candidates with unique offerings—those previously shut out from admissions—are filling the college campuses.

DOI: 10.4324/9781003380948-3

As an applicant, it is important to ask how campuses have specif-ically adapted to such things as health protocols and admissions changes, and candidates should seek this info in relation to any col-leges they are exploring or considering.

All things relating to COVID-19 have transformed and shaped the entire college admissions—the biggest being larger-than-ever test-optional admissions and applicant review process. COVID-19 has also impacted the going-to-college aspect and living on campus. Key aspects such as deferring acceptances to taking a gap year in 2019/2020 and 2020/2021 have impacted future application years with respect to enrollment numbers and acceptance availabilities at many colleges due to a surge in numbers of applicants and transfer students, etc. In some cases, colleges have oversubscribed accep-tances and overenrolled the most recent applicant year (which could also be further exacerbated by next-year deferral entrances), creating an even smaller admissions year for applicants in the rising applicant pool.

Some colleges have oversubscribed their enrollment by extend-ing offers beyond their typical rising class numbers, but we must remember the sheer number of applicants has increased despite COVID-19 due to some very important reasons such as a surplus of colleges adopting a test-optional admissions process and the ease of applying to numerous colleges at once with the entrance of the common[1] and coalition application[2] platforms. Because of this ease, the average number of college applications per student is on the rise, whereas the average number of college applications stands between seven to ten colleges.

Application simplification, a platform of first-ever test-optional institutions, and a result of an influx of applications, colleges are seeing healthier and more competitive applicant pools surfacing, and larger-than-ever numbers of applications have flooded the col-lege review committees' desks. Positively speaking, test-optional surges falling out in response to COVID's many shutdowns have attracted so many new candidates to colleges that otherwise (prior to COVID) would not have been considered due to their test scores alone. Colleges are seeing a whole new, refreshing applicant pool.

NOTES

1 Common App is a nonprofit membership organization that supports all students, and those who support them, through the college admission process.
2 The Coalition for College, formerly the Coalition for Access, Affordability, and Success, is an American nonprofit organization that runs the Coalition Application, a US college application platform.

KEY TAKEAWAYS

COVID-19 has created natural shifts in all aspects of the college landscape: research, planning, visitation, candidate review, acceptance numbers, and matriculation.

Response to COVID-19 protocols has impacted key campus responses to living and learning. Many colleges have adopted a test-optional admissions position changing the types and numbers of applicants seen in one application cycle.

Colleges have adapted protocols in place to respond to varying levels of active and passive COVID-19 through notification systems, vaccine policies, and distance learning, to name a few.

Students are encouraged to investigate the college's protocols in place throughout these ever-changing landscapes.

Some colleges have faced waxing and waning enrollment numbers due to a variety of factors.

TWO-YEAR VS.
FOUR-YEAR COLLEGES

Let me start by identifying my use of "institutions" which refers to all colleges and universities, both private and public, two-year as well as four-year.

Students, your choice to attend a two-year college—community colleges—can be a cost-effective decision as well as a time-saver, especially when it comes to completing basic 100-level general education requisites in preparation for transfer to a four-year college to pursue a bachelor's degree. At the community college level, many associate degree programs can be completed within two years.

Many in-state private and public universities have transfer articulation agreements with the state's local community colleges, meaning they will allow transfer from an associate degree program to the four-year institution and enroll as a junior.

See your School Counselor for additional local information, as memorandums of understanding, and transferability of credits may differ within state, and certainly differ from state-to-state.

Students, it is common to not yet know what major you wish to explore. Perhaps, too, you are finding that your undergrad grades, GPA, and overall transcript are not what they need to be for admission consideration.

BENEFITS OF ATTENDING A COMMUNITY COLLEGE
AS OPPOSED TO A FOUR-YEAR UNIVERSITY

Do you feel that you are not as academically prepared to take on the challenges of a four-year academic program of studies as, perhaps,

DOI: 10.4324/9781003380948-4

your peers? Do you think you may benefit from an additional year of growth and maturity before you tackle college life and independence on a four-year campus? You are not alone. Enrolling at a community college can offer benefits such as flexibility in gaining life experiences, saving time and money, navigating and exploring various academic courses before choosing a major, and building an academically strong transcript.

How can a community college experience help you prepare for a four-year college program? You may find that while you are academically prepared to attend a four-year college, you may need more time to grow, mature, and experience life before settling into a full-time college program. Don't panic—many students may show apprehension about taking this leap into college life. You may not be ready to live on your own just yet. Perhaps your academic record does not reflect your academic ability or commitment to study. In this case, taking college courses here and there to build stamina and a going-to-college routine can improve your level of independence and increase your self-confidence. Academically, taking community college courses takes grit and determination. By doing so, you are on your way to building an academic record at the college level— this may be just what you need to prove your readiness to attend larger institutions. You may benefit from the flexible offerings of community college to demonstrate a great potential to tackle the college's rigorous and fast-paced program of studies. Maybe you have a job during the day and prefer to take classes at night. Community colleges offer flexibility in the frequency and delivery method of course offerings. There is likely a program that can work with your specific needs.

You may identify as a student who typically shines in the classroom. Yet, due to recent or resurfacing emotional impact, your success is impeded. Perhaps you are restricted medically or physically and cannot venture onto a self-sustaining campus without the monitoring and support of family, friends, or more critical levels of interventional and therapeutic entities. Entering a smaller, more manageable commuter campus may offer the physical environment necessary to provide comfort and safety to meet your needs.

PERSONAL SETBACKS

You may identify as a student battling a mental health illness or mental health episode or one who has in the past. Perhaps you need consistent, intensive emotional support and time to outfit yourself for a rewarding and independent life on campus. Taking a class or two at your local community college will bolster opportunities to build resiliency and self-confidence and the chance to earn credit and build a healthy academic record for when you are healthy and ready to transfer to a four-year institution.

Wherever you land on this topic, there are sound reasons to consider attending a two-year community college.

Other benefits of applying to two-year institutions range from no-SAT® or ACT® score requirements, rolling admissions deadlines which, based on enrollment capacities, extend the possibility of applying late into your senior year (e.g., June or July) so long as there are availabilities on campus for additional students. This is a great option for students who had applied in the fall but may not have been accepted to their first lists of colleges; or for those that, due to finances, need to change course. Rolling admissions is also very amenable to those "late starters" to the college application process.

Some final perks to enrolling at a community college are flexibility and time management for students who wish to or need to work for income purposes. Course offerings are usually plentiful and offer numerous semesters including one or two summer sessions, which allows for greater planning and flexibility to better balance work, school, and life expectations.

Financially speaking, courses are less expensive than those at a four-year institution. Community colleges' fee per credit ranges anywhere from just over $200 per credit. According to Maryland's Montgomery College, the total cost of tuition decreases per credit hour total, meaning the more credits obtained, the lower the cost per credit (Montgomery College).

A first-year tuition may range between $1300–$6800, depending on the state (Hanson, 2021).

Beyond the deadline, financial, and transferability benefits listed earlier, students can benefit from attending a two-year college if they are trialing out the college experience or balancing work and academic demands. Community college courses can be taken and paid for in a "pay-as-you-go" format—one class here, another there, instead of enrolling in a full-semester course load.

REFERENCES

Melanie Hanson. "Average Cost of Community College." Education Data Initiative at educationdata.org, December 27, 2021. https://educationdata.org/average-cost-of-community-college.

Montgomery College. "Current Tuition Rates." www.montgomerycollege.edu. www.montgomerycollege.edu/paying-for-college/tuition/current-rates.html#montgomerycountyresidents.

KEY TAKEAWAYS

Two-year colleges offer the following benefits:

Seamless transfer articulation agreements between same in-state institutions to a four-year institution
Offer flexible enrollment options
Do not require SAT®/ACT® testing
Costs per credit are fractional compared with four-year institutions
Many two-year institutions offer full associate degree programs
Offer work/academic/life demands balance
Offer opportunity to improve academics

ALTERNATIVE POST-SECONDARY PURSUITS—CONSIDERING A GAP YEAR, IMMERSION PROGRAMS, TRAVEL ABROAD, OR FULL-YEAR COLLEGE DEFERMENTS

WHAT IS GAP YEAR?

A gap year is a year taken in between the end of secondary schooling and the beginning of post-secondary, or college, education. It is a break from academics—a time for students to discover more of themselves and decide what it is that they wish to pursue for a college experience and academic major. The time allotted (usually a year) in areas other than matriculation into a college can be spent in a variety of ways: travel, work, volunteering, internship, or peace or mission work.

Gap years have increased in popularity over the years, especially considering COVID. There is a growing understanding and overall acceptance of creating a pause between high school and college, and there are many good reasons some may be considering a pause.

The rationale mainly is that students may have felt their initial first year college experience may be short-changed, as COVID and its related restrictions have placed a damper on the otherwise carefree and unrestricted vibrance of college life and all things typical of campus life as known to all others before COVID. A gap year would otherwise afford a student a buffer year between

DOI: 10.4324/9781003380948-5

high school and first-year college enrollment with a structured delayed start.

MENTAL HEALTH RECHARGE

I have emphasized mental and physical health in my introduction as well as throughout in **Chapters 3, 18,** and again in **25.** Balance and health are key factors in the consideration of one taking a gap year. Students have faced a tumultuous challenge in light of COVID, from higher competition and lower admit rates in the college arena, to socialization, to the loss of academic progress, and getting back into the fast-paced programming has been a challenge. Students may take this gap year to heal and adjust.

Parents are also accepting of the possibility that their student may not jump right away into college. Perhaps they too are seeing the need for a pause, and as a result, we are seeing more and more agencies and outfits that are meeting this need.

ACCEPTED BUT PLAN TO TAKE A GAP YEAR? GET ORGANIZED AND PLAN

Now *structured* is the key word here. If you are considering taking a gap year, you'll want to have an organized and well-planned use for this year. There is no just sitting around at home. It's important to showcase your continued demonstrated commitment to self-learning and exploration, growth, and continued advancement of self throughout this year.

Get organized. If you are a student who intends to take a gap year, and one who has successfully completed the college application process and has received an acceptance to one or more colleges, then you may wish to accept but defer to your colleges of choice. By doing so, you are reserving your spot as a matriculating student in the year to come, not the immediate fall semester. This is honestly the easier, more prepared route to take than the one subsequently.

HOLDING OFF ON APPLYING? NEXT STEPS

However, if you are a student who has not and will very likely not apply this year for fall admission, but instead take on a gap year and then apply to colleges, then work with your school counselor to secure the following items before you leave high school:

- ☐ Maximize your time spent in a gap year—plan, plan, plan, and make use of this time and experience
- ☐ Take an SAT or ACT
- ☐ Obtain letters of recommendation from at least two academic teachers; and one from your school counselor
- ☐ Articulate your plans to your teachers/counselor and ask if they would write on your behalf for college applications a year from now
- ☐ Seek a more recent LOR from a professor, employer, internship supervisor, or travel organization, as this will speak to your gap year credentials and serve as a most recent depiction of your growth
- ☐ Decide if a postgrad (PG) year is better for you to boost your grades; course rigor and athletic ability as demonstrated by an additional year of athletic showcasing before participating in NCAA collegiate levels DI and DII

KEY TAKEAWAYS

Gap years offer unique self-learning, explorative experiences commenced immediately post high school and pre-college duration.

Gap years have grown in popularity—especially in response to COVID impacts to the application and college life experiences, as students often took a pause on matriculating to college to experience a fuller, more typical college life experience all around.

Get organized. Get all college application docs completed, including letters of recommendation, before you leave high school.

If deferring from a college acceptance, then seek to obtain any NEW letters of recommendation, if needed.

If attending a PG (postgraduate) year for the purpose of athletics or academic improvement, then follow the traditional college application process outlined by PG college or school counselor.

PART 2

HOW TO APPLY?

COMMON-, COALITION-, INSTITUTION-BASED APPLICATIONS

What and how do they matter?

Common App[1] (a common application among over 1000 colleges and universities), or "CA," as indicated on Naviance (a college and career planning tool), and the Coalition Application (CO or CoA as indicated on Naviance) are two popular college application consortiums through which students apply to colleges. (Common App is a nonprofit membership organization that supports all students, and those who support them, through the college admission process.)

Both Naviance® and Scoir® as well as many other college research and planning software platforms, as referenced earlier, can aid in the organizational process of college applicants and required materials. I am most familiar with Naviance, so that will be the most-referred platform throughout this guide when applicable. Once you enter your colleges of choice into Naviance's *Colleges I am Applying to* list, the program identifies the application type (or admissions type) along with the application deadline and incidentals, such as the number of letters of recommendation accepted. This is important as some colleges will not accept more than one, whereas some will accept up to four, but many institutions will not even accept any. For more information on these aspects, refer to **Chapter 14: Value of the LORs (letters of recommendation).**

At the time of writing this publication, over 900 institutions make up the Common App consortium, while 150 institutions are part of the Coalition Application movement. All, but one college, remain dually part of Coalition and Common App platforms or Common App and institution-based application providing a choice

DOI: 10.4324/9781003380948-7

for the applicant on how to apply. University of Washington (UWA) is self-standing as a Coalition-exclusive university, meaning it will only accept an application through the Coalition system.

You are encouraged to search the application tool approved for use by the college so that you are prepared to complete the appropriate application method preferred by the institution. In the interest of time and ease, it is recommended that you, as the future applicant, apply by the method that reaches the most on your list. This will not only help organize the application process but it will also pare down the amount of time spent on completing the document itself.

No matter the application type submitted, there are universal application requirements for all students across some, if not all, colleges on a typical student applicant's list: official high school transcript, official SAT® or ACT® score reports (ordered and sent from the testing agencies, not the high school), letters of recommendations, application fee, essay(s) and/or a personal statement. Some colleges will also accept a résumé listing employment and/or volunteer experiences and extracurricular activities. **Also see Chapter 15: Social media and email etiquette.**

NOTE

1   Common App is a nonprofit membership organization that supports all students, and those who support them, through the college admission process.

 ## KEY TAKEAWAYS

Various vehicles in which to apply: Common-, Coalition-, and institution-based applications.

Colleges will indicate which application and method is preferred.

College and career planning programs such as Naviance® and Scoir® help to organize the application processes for students (indicating application type, date, method, and application requirements such as a letter of recommendation, per college).

Help organize the student applicant by choosing the best, most efficient method of application to organize and complete the process.

DATA-DRIVEN SCHOOLS VS. HOLISTIC

Two divergent admissions review processes split by means of how a student is reviewed for admission into a college or university. Simply divided, it is safe to say that most large-scale public universities are data-driven in their review process. Meaning, application review committees ranging from one to two people upwards of 20 score a student's application based on key components referred to as hard and soft factors. These data points, quantitative and qualitative, serve as informative factors in the review and consideration of an applicant for admissions. Hard factors": grades, GPA, types, and levels of classes taken (course rigor), standardized test scores; and "soft factors": extracurricular activities, letters of recommendation, strength of high school, essay(s), personal statement, and demonstrated interest together paint a picture of the preparedness and appropriateness of a candidate for admission. They speak to the overall fit quality that institutions are seeking. (See demonstrated interests subsection later) (Ivywise.com: www. ivywise.com/blog/how-college-applications-are-evaluated-the-soft-factors/). Now the earlier listing is in somewhat of a purposeful and narrative order. Most colleges seeking all these items will rank the preference level of each of these items that apply into their application review committee process.

Institutions that partake in data-driven review processes are those that will exclusively rely on empirical data and review GPA, rank, test scores, course selection, and rigor, while not considering letters of recommendation nor personal essays. Data-driven review institutions receive upwards of 20,000 applications a year for anywhere

DOI: 10.4324/9781003380948-8

between 2,000 and 3,000 enrollment vacancies. These institutions do not have the time nor the means to read multiple essays nor conduct multiple rounds of review for each candidate. Instead, they utilize data metrics as predictors of on-campus, in-learning success. Data hosts predictive power of academic preparedness and fit, but one can argue whether it also informs culture and climate campus fit as well.

Colleges that utilize a holistic review process—typically private selective institutions who also may receive a more proportionate number of applications to ratio of available seats—will review the applicant from a 360-degree perspective, meaning all the parts making up that person—hard factors: grades, courses rigor, class placement; and soft factors: essays, letters of recommendation, extracurricular activities, and personal interests.

DEMONSTRATED INTERESTS

While not all colleges will track nor consider demonstrated interest, there are some that consider it a strong factor in its admissions process. For example, American University, Quinnipiac University, Cooper Union, US Naval and Air Force Academies, and others who consider interest to some degree: Denison, High Point, Lehigh, Roanoke College, William & Mary, Howard University, to name a few. Others who do not weigh interest into consideration: Florida State, James Madison, MIT, UCal system, Temple, and University of Virginia (UVA), etc.

Here are some other ways to demonstrate interest in a college or specific program: do college visits, open, read, and reply to emails sent from colleges, highlight and respond to college social media posts or activities; but remember to keep replies professional, connect via virtual tours or alum chats, ask for an informal interview, and attend rep visits at school.

REFERENCE

Ivywise.com. www.ivywise.com/blog/how-college-applications-are-evaluated-the-soft-factors/ (November 9, 2017).

KEY TAKEAWAYS

Two divergent admissions review processes split by means of *how* a student is reviewed for admission into a college or university: holistic review and data-driven review.

Most large-scale public universities are data-driven in their review process.

Holistic review includes both hard (quantitative) and soft factors (qualitative).

ADMISSION TYPES AND DEADLINES

Varying deadline options offers flexibility for some applicants and can allow for one to stagger application commitments across varying deadlines; yet, with the ease of Common App, especially, the process of applying to many colleges at one time regardless of their varying deadlines has never been easier. Overall, there is a growing trend for students to apply early as a mode of completing the application process. There are benefits to applying via an early application window which will be detailed further later in this chapter. Here's a quick breakdown of the varying admissions types offered by some colleges. Quick tip: not every college will offer every type mentioned subsequently. It is important for student applicants to discover which application type(s) each listed college offers.

REGULAR ADMISSION

Regular Admissions is one of the most Common App types with varying deadlines. Colleges will indicate a set date at which all applications and accompanying materials will be received by the college so that they may be considered for admission. Applicants can certainly apply before the deadline has been reached, but those latecomers are out of luck as, once the deadline has been reached, late applicants have officially missed the deadline. It is very likely that the admissions review of applications will not begin until the day after the marked deadline has been reached.

DOI: 10.4324/9781003380948-9

ROLLING ADMISSION

Rolling admissions is the opposite of regular deadline as it does not hold any type of deadline. In fact, colleges will accept applications at the beginning in the late summer of one's high school senior year up through mid to late spring. Colleges will accept applications and continue to accept students so long as there are availabilities within the entering class. It is beneficial to apply on the earlier side of the application window than later as, depending upon the popularity of the institution, program, or intended major, slots may start out in limited number and may fill quickly. Also, for rolling admissions schools, you may hear back from your college within six to eight weeks, which can relieve some fears and anxieties about the never-ending wait.

EARLY ACTION AND EARLY DECISION

Early action (EA) and early decision (EA) types are very popular. The benefit of early is that student applicants receive a decision on the earlier side as well—usually within four to eight weeks. Although some institutions impose neither application type nor deadline, many do, and it is crucial to note there is one key difference between the two. Early decision is a binding agreement made through a written articulation agreement between the student/family and institution that, if accepted, one will attend. By applying early decision, one is making a commitment to the college that they will attend so long as their base financial need has been met via the various monies determined by the financial aid office: grants, scholarships, loans, work-study, to name a few.

Early decision (ED) is appropriate for some, but certainly not all applicants. Some will say ED is for those that want to marry their school. If accepted via early decision, a student must retract all applications to all other colleges. Most early action and early decision deadlines are November 1 (while a few institutions impose an earlier early deadline of October 1 or 15). Institutions may also offer two early decision windows via early decision I or early decision II. Students who are applying via early decision are those for whom the university is their top choice; usually, a highly selective one (low admissions percentage), or program of choice is highly selective and restrictive, for example, a prestigious honors program, competitive program, or major and for which finances and affordability have been heavily discussed and contemplated. While students can apply to as many colleges with an early action deadline, they can only choose one college to which to apply via early decision. Some students may be able to apply early decision I or II to a college and then, if denied admissions, can then apply to a set of colleges accepting applications in the regular deadline, or rolling admissions deadline window. A clever student may be able to apply to one top institution via early decision I (11/1) window, for example, Boston University, and then apply to a second top choice college via an early decision II deadline (1/15), or even in February, for example, Occidental College if they are denied from admissions to their first choice. Colleges have added early decision II to their admissions cycle to further impact their yield as they know top students may be denied admission to their first choices. Students can also take advantage of this later window to improve SAT® or ACT® scores as well as grades while also benefiting from the more favorable review process at a highly selective institution.

Admissions options and related contingencies can get tricky at some more select institutions such as Yale, Princeton, and Notre Dame which offer variations of an early acceptance application referred to as *Single-Choice Early Action* or *Restricted Early Action*. These variations may exclude or restrict applicants from applying early to *any* other (in most cases, private) institution either via early action or early decision, such as in the case of Princeton University. Yet Yale will allow a student to apply for other public institutions' early action II or early decision II deadlines and any college with a rolling admissions program as well as any international institution. Notre Dame furthers the allowance, stating that students can apply to early action programs offered by any other institution, as well as any institution with early decision II deadlines.

Benefits of applying early extend beyond just learning of a college's decision early. For example, the acceptability rate, meaning the speed and process of which colleges are accepting students, is higher and more likely during the earlier windows so long as candidates are nearing or meeting the admissions criteria, as institutions are looking to fill as much of their annual admissions yield, which means the number of students who accept to enroll in the fall based on those number of those acceptances that the institution has made. For example, if a college makes 1000 acceptances and 650 students accept the college's decision to enroll; therefore, a 65% yield. "Bates College, for example, admits 70% of their freshman class through the ED I [and] II cycles. . . . They all, like thousands of other schools, show extra love to applicants who pledge attendance" (Belasco, 2022). Since most students apply via the early action or decision application cycle, colleges are banking on filling in as much of their yield as possible, realizing that the number of applicants would likely decrease as the year progresses and the application window ends (Data source credited to: Jennie Kent and Jeff Levy, 2020).

Deciding whether early decision or early action is right for you? The answer may be neither. Early decision commitment may be too imposing and risky for some, whereas early action may not be binding; it may be too aggressive a deadline that a student feels rushed. While some earlier deadlines suggest a larger acceptance percentage, this is not the case for all colleges. For example, Northeastern University's early decision acceptance rate is 51%, meaning 51 out of 100 students who applied via early decision were accepted. If all those accepted ED were to enroll, they would make up 22% of the freshman class admitted as ED candidates, whereas 77% would be filled by candidates from the regular decision pool. In contrast, Ramapo College of New Jersey accepts 80% of applications through the ED window, but this drawn population pool only encompasses the enrolling class by 12%. Claremont McKenna's (CA) ED acceptance rate is 29%, and if all were to enroll, they would represent 56% of the enrolling freshman class (Kent and Levy, 2022).

PLAN AHEAD

Some things to consider when planning your application list and once you've determined the deadline choices that you are committing to. Do yourself and your school counselor a favor and get your applications, essays, supplemental components, and all requirements for your "backup" plans completed before Thanksgiving. For many reasons, getting through the application process before the major holidays will bring you peace of mind so that you have plans A, B, and C completed. For example, submit your apps for 11/1 early action or early decision; but if you are deferred or rejected, your second-tier college apps and their supplements are already ready to go. If you are lucky to be accepted to your ED college, then your process is completed; however, if you chose early action colleges, and acceptances start to populate, you can wait to choose where to attend. Perhaps, wait for the financial aid packages to arrive. Yet, if none of your college acceptances come forth, or with the financial aid that you need, you may be finding yourself pulling all the stops for your third-tier colleges. If done ahead of time, you've just saved yourself time. Waiting into the holidays gets you into trouble. Your counseling office is closed; no one can send transcripts and letters of recommendation over the holidays. You're off from school—so too are your school counselors. Simply put, plan ahead.

REFERENCES

Andrew Belasco. "Colleges That Offer Early Decision 2." College Transition, September 14, 2022. www.collegetransitions.com/blog/early-decision-ii/.

Jennie Kent and Jeff Levy. "Early Decision and Regular Decision Acceptance Rates—Class of 2023." Big J Educational Consulting, August 2020. www.bigjeducationalconsulting.com/resources.

Jennie Kent and Jeff Levy. "Early Decision and Regular Decision Acceptance Rates—Class of 2025." August 2022. www.bigjeducationalconsulting.com/resources.

 ## KEY TAKEAWAYS

There are four most popular application types: early action, early decision, rolling admissions, and regular deadline.

Early decision is binding; one must retract applications from all other colleges if accepted to the college via early decision.

Complete all college application components before the holidays—Thanksgiving, if possible, but no later than 12/15.

Be prepared for various decision outcomes, and have all items completed to enact plans A, B, and C.

8

THE WAVE OF SELECTIVITY
Reach, target, and safety

The goal set forth by all school counselors and others assisting students with the college application process is to impress upon you the need to create a list of colleges that covers the full spectrum of selectivity and, therefore, likelihood of an acceptance. *Reach, target,* and *safety* (or better said, "likely") schools represent the three categories of colleges making up this spectrum.

REACH

A reach school is one that a student is very unlikely to get into. They have admissions rates of 3–8%, and they are reach schools for nearly every student. This does not mean that no one will be accepted, as, remember, between 3% and 8% are accepted, but 92% to 97% are not. These top selective schools are known as the "Ivies" or Ivy League institutions: Princeton, Brown University, New York University (NYU), Yale, Harvard, Carnegie Mellon, Stamford, and Swarthmore, to name a few. Other less selective, but still incredibly selective, campuses known as mini Ivy Leagues: Amherst, Colby, Bates, Bowdoin, Connecticut College, and Colgate, to name a few. Schools at this reach level may look different for everyone, unless the reach schools that are non-guarantees for 100% of all applicants, in which case usually refers to those with single-digit admission rates.

TARGET

A target school is one at which a student has a pretty good chance of being accepted, and with comfortability at stake, I say a pretty

DOI: 10.4324/9781003380948-10

good chance may equate to a 40–60% chance. Whereas a student may not meet all or most of the qualifying admissions criteria, there is a greater chance of acceptance than certainly at an Ivy League or reach school. A list of target schools will look remarkably different for all candidates based on grades, GPA, skillset, activities, special interests, SAT®/ACT® scores, etc.

SAFETY

A safety school is just what its name implies—a surer fit and one usually in the "green light" accepted zone. Although there are no guarantees in this world, safety schools do offer a sense of reassurance of a greater likelihood of being accepted than target schools and, certainly, reach schools. Acceptance rates are nearing 75–100%. These are colleges that, again, will look different for each candidate but may consist of community colleges for some or a private liberal arts and otherwise selective school for others. Much like target schools, the list of safety schools will differ among students. What might be a safety school for one student might be a moderately selective target, or even a reach school, for another.

DIVERSIFY YOUR LIST

One overarching and extremely important piece of the adage is: do not put your eggs in one basket (Miguel Cervantes 1605 Don Quixote) [author's note: There is some controversy over the origin of the phrase "Don't put all your eggs in one basket," although the expression is most commonly attributed to Miguel Cervantes (Miguel de Cervantes Saavedra, 1986 [1547–1616].), I've borrowed his meaning, in this case, to include avoiding having a list of colleges heavily representing the reach category while only having one target college and perhaps no safety schools. Remember, you want your list to be fully representative of each of the three selectivity ranges; however, you do not need to have a list of a million and one colleges either. The average application list consists of four to seven colleges.

Another important note, and one that cannot go without saying, keep all colleges on your list that meet your interests and that qualifies as a good fit. Get rid of any, and all colleges, that, if presented as the only option for you, would destroy you as a person and make you miserable. Get rid of it—scratch it off your list and toss it into oblivion. There is no need to have a college on your list for that would make you miserable should it be the only option in the end. Also, moms, dads, cousins, guardians, uncles, grandma, mom-moms, and pop-pops, this is your [state your affiliation to the student applicant]'s college experience, not, and I repeat, NOT YOUR EXPERIENCE. Therefore, do not pressure your student into applying to a college because it is where you attended 30-plus years ago. A lot has changed since then. Trust me. A lot.

REFERENCE

Miguel de Cervantes Saavedra. *The Adventures of Don Quixote De La Mancha*. New York: Farrar, Straus, Giroux, 1986 [1547–1616].

KEY TAKEAWAYS

There are three types of colleges across the spectrum of selectivity: reach, target, and safety.

Safety does not guarantee an acceptance, but it surely increases the likelihood, depending on a student's credentials.

A college list does not need to be extensive, but it should cover the three categories of colleges.

A college list needs to have a backup college, but one that a student would be happy to attend if it becomes the only option.

Do not apply to a college just because someone told you to; you must have an interest in the institution.

Balance is key.

Aim of the stars, but also plan for more realistic options.

No one size fits all for all students.

Everyone's list will differ.

9

WHEN TO TEST, WHAT TO TEST, HOW MANY TIMES?

The decision to register for and take either the SAT® or ACT® or both is a personal decision likely fueled by peer pressure, natural assumption, and requirements imposed by colleges and universities. The rationale used in arriving at a choice is becoming clearer even among the cloud cover of an over-testing atmosphere. Since COVID, a blessed thing has occurred from the vantage point of college admissions and the applicant: colleges have relaxed or eliminated their standardized exams from their entrance requirements and application review processes. Phew, right? Well, also among this decision comes the onslaught of applications from those who might not have otherwise applied should the institution's testing policy remain intact. The two testing agencies: College Board and its SAT®, and the ACT® dominate the entrance landscape for applicants. These exams do not come at a breezy cost, but rather they get quite pricey, especially if you decide to take the exam numerous times. Topping $60 a pop, these agencies bring in a boatload of money annually through test administration. Colleges and changes made to their enrollment processes and criteria no doubt buckled the knees of these bureaus, but the was a long time coming, as many colleges have either been on the brink of removing standardized testing from their review regiment, and COVID was the necessary push needed to commit to such a movement, or colleges had preceded COVID in their decision to do away with test scores as they felt other standardized and empirical data points were just as compelling to predict academic preparedness and success on campus as any other data-metric exam. In fact, close to over 1600 colleges now have moved into the category of test-optional, meaning standardized

DOI: 10.4324/9781003380948-11

test scores are no longer required, and, in some cases, test-blind, meaning test scores, if submitted, will not be reviewed in any case. Fairtest.org is the central hub listing all colleges and universities which do not require SAT® or ACT® at all. This list now has over 1800 institutions: a marked increase since pre-COVID, which stood around 900.

TO SUBMIT OR NOT TO SUBMIT YOUR SCORES

There are two growing fields of thought on whether students should submit scores or proceed as test-optional candidates. One camp feels that if students are meeting the threshold of the median (middle 50%) of recommended SAT®/ACT® scores, then submit those scores, while another growing camp is stating not to submit scores if not in the upper echelon of ranges. What is expected is that those who have near-perfect to perfect scores will be sending scores to colleges, so those that are not meeting this percentile may wish to consider not sending scores. A student's question usually falls into the context of, if I am considering sending scores, what score is a good score for this specific college? The answers to this question will vary among institutions or even go so far as to vary among college programs within the large context university. Generally, if a student is not representing scores in the top 50–75th percentile (the upper two quartiles), then there is a heavy recommendation to not submit scores.

Here is an example of a Common Data Profile for Tulane University's 2019–2020 class.

From this data bar, we see that an SAT® score below 1400 falls to the bottom quarter (or "quartile") of SAT® ranges among students admitted to Tulane during the 2022–2023 admission cycle. Meanwhile, a score above 1500 falls to the top quartile. The middle 50% of admitted students attained SAT® scores in the 1370 to 1480 range, and we can estimate the midpoint to be 1450. In 2022, 50% of first-time, first-year (freshmen) students had an SAT® score between 1400–1600.

It is generally strongly advised of students to submit test scores when accessing above the midpoint or median range of the college's posted SAT®/ACT® profile, meaning that students are falling within the college's top two quartile brackets. Those in the bottom

Table 9.1 Common Data Profile for Tulane University's 2022–2023 class

	25th percentile	*75th percentile*
SAT® Composite	1400	1450
SAT® EBRW	680	720
SAT® Math	690	730
ACT® Composite	31	32
ACT® Math	27	29
ACT® English	32	34

★ ★ ★

Bottom Quartile <1370	Third Quartile 1370–1420	Second Quartile 1430–1480	Top Quartile >1490

Source: Format of grid sourced from: www.applerouth.com/blog/2020/10/27/to-submit-or-not-to-submit-the-test-optional-dilemma/Data sourced from public record Common Data Set https://tulane.app.box.com/s/r53izqi0eq9dpkt0hwqwzlcahe2g9ooa

quartiles (25th–50th percentiles, or bottom half) are strongly advised to not submit test scores. Of course, there are stronger recommendations to hold on submitting test scores if one is not in the top 75th–99th percentiles, nearing those scores of 1480+ if one is applying for selectively competitive programs such as engineering, nursing, computer science, data science, finance, and in some colleges, even psychology carries a highly restrictive placement rate and class size, which creates more competitive and selective review process.

Powerful, yet limited, data gathered and presented by various authors, such as Jed Applerouth, PhD and Peter Wischusen (2022), carefully presents that for some institutions lies a possibility for test-submitter advantage. Public and readily available institutional data—retrievable through *public common data set* information reported by the higher education community and compiled by publishers supported by college awareness and research institutions—indicates that for some institutions, test submitters may have had an unclear advantage for admissions over those that had not submitted scores.

While this breadth of information is limited and does not cast a wide net, but rather on a small cluster of 11 rather selective and highly selective colleges, the assumption of data and its meaning must be taken lightly. However, there are institutions, otherwise, listed as test-optional where it is likely that test-submitter advantage may exist. For example, Boston College's admission rate for those that applied with test scores for the class of 2022 was 29%; whereas the admit rate fell below the overall college's general admissions rate of 19%, at just 11% for those who applied without submitting test scores. This indicates that Boston College applicants have a 169% greater chance of acceptance with the submission of test scores. Now what this doesn't tell is what those scores were, despite the common data set indicating the median score and average test scores for the middle 50% of those that applied. It is suggested that likely those that generally submitted scores are those with the highest performance—likely within the recommended top 75th–99th percentiles. In comparison, Vanderbilt, with a general admission rate of only 7% shed no discretionary difference in admissions likelihood among those test submitters (7%) and those not (6%).

SAT® VS. ACT®

The SAT® and ACT® have a lot of similarities such as price, timing, essay component, no reduction of points for wrong answers, use of a calculator on one or more mathematics section(s), multiple-choice format, score cancellation option, and common universality of acceptance of either/both exams by colleges; but each test has distinct differences worth noting.

The SAT®, which stands for scholastic aptitude test, purely means that it tests areas of unknown familiarity and concept acquisition for the pure sake of assessing one's likelihood of accuracy based on deductive reasoning skills, decoding, and interpretation of material. While the SAT® will test areas of content that may not have been covered in a student's curriculum at that time, the ACT® is said to be more closely aligned with current grade-level content. Meaning, the ACT® will test concepts that most closely align with current classroom content and curriculum likely acquired in one's content courses.

Table 9.2 Other Key Differences: SAT® vs. ACT® Comparison Table

	SAT®	ACT®
Scoring Scale	200–800 2 main sections (4 parts): 200–800 points each = 1600 **Average: 1060**	0–36 4 sections: 1–36 points each. **Average: 20**
Subtest Areas	Math, Evidenced-based Reading; Essay—discontinued	Math, Evidenced-based Reading, Science, History, and Optional Essay
Math	Lots of trig/algebra II	Lots of geometry
Science	No science (but two math sections)	Science, one math section
Retest Opportunities	Yes, full test only	Yes, per section
English Essay	Longer essay passages; more analysis	Shorter passages, offer own perspective
Essay	Discontinued as of January 2021	Yes
Answer Choices	Four	Five
Time per Question	one minute, ten seconds	36 seconds to one minute
Testing Accommodations	Yes, once approved, approved for all exam registrations	Yes, must be requested and approved at time of each exam registration
Testing Date Administrations	August, October, November, December, March, May, and June	September, October, December, February, April, and June
Changes for 2023–2024	Digital testing will be replacing paper and pen/pencil testing starting in the fall of 2023 (paper testing will no longer be available starting spring 2024). Also, the test is getting shorter—down to two hours from three hours.	Currently paper and digital platforms

The SAT® and ACT® each has a reading comprehension/reasoning test section and a mathematics section. While the SAT®'s mathematics is heavily concentrated on algebra and a smaller focus on geometry, the ACT® is heavily focused on geometry, trigonometry, and functions. A formula sheet is provided on the SAT®, but not the ACT®. Some of the key anatomical sections of these two tests are outlined subsequently.

REFERENCE

Jed Applerouth and Peter Wischusen. "Do Test Scores Give and Admissions Advantage?" July 12, 2022. www.applerouth.com/blog/2022/07/12/do-students-with-test-scores-have-an-admissions-advantage-what-we-know-and-what-we-dont/

KEY TAKEAWAYS

Students should consult their colleges' websites to determine the application requirements.

Many colleges do not require standardized tests. Some are test-optional, test-flexible, or test-blind.

The two standardized exams are SAT® and ACT®.

These tests are normed and are reliable over time, meaning the more a student tests, the more similar and consistent are their test scores.

There is no magic answer to the number or type of tests one should take and if one should take one over the other, or any at all.

Limited data suggests that for some colleges, the test-submitter advantage may exist.

Counselors recommend students submit test scores if they represent within the top 75th–99th percentile of the college's listed SAT®/ ACT® scores but to withhold or exercise the test-optional method if scores are below this range. This is exceptionally recommended for highly selective colleges and/or competitive programs.

Most often, those who choose to test will take the SAT® or ACT® no more than two times.

- The ACT® and SAT® are universally accepted by all institutions accepting standardized assessment scores. There is no test preference.
- The SAT® and ACT® have many similarities but also have key content and structure differences that may help a student in deciding which test to take.

10

SELF-REPORTED ACADEMIC RECORD (SRAR©/SSAR©)

So you've applied to your list of colleges by way of Common App or the institution's application found on its website or the Coalition application, or perhaps you've utilized a combination across each of these tools. God bless if you fall into this category, but hold onto your seat—as there's more!

SSAR-SRAR-©

Just when you thought you were done. Here comes the moment that you now need to transcribe your official transcript into the online portal of those colleges requiring a self-reporting academic record. For the purposes of this chapter, I will refer to the self-reporting tool acronym, SSAR-SRAR-©. The two once-independent academic reporting vehicles (SSAR and SRAR) have merged, according to the SSAR's notation in their access site: your SSAR account is the same beginning August 1, 2022. Each of your three years' worth of courses, final average grades from each, total credit received in each course, and an accurate list of your current courses in your senior year will need to be loaded into your college's applicant portal. Here's how best to navigate this. Make sure that you confirm those colleges on your list that require the SSAR-SRAR (2023). Which colleges/universities accept the SRAR? https://scarletcs.zendesk.com/hc/en-us/articles/360024423094-Which-colleges-universities-accept-the-SRAR©

DOI: 10.4324/9781003380948-12

NAVIGATING SELF-REPORTING

One, pay attention to deadlines! Much like the initial application deadline, say 11/1, there will also be a SRAR deadline. It's usually anywhere from two weeks to a month after the initial application deadline. If you miss the SRAR deadline, you are out of luck. Colleges infer a failed receipt of the SRAR as a student no longer being interested in their institution. Do not let this seal your fate.

Kindly ask your school counselor for a copy (does not need to be official) of your high school transcript reflecting all courses taken, their final grades, and credits earned per course. Make sure your current senior year courses are confirmed. You do not want to report that you are enrolled in AP® Computer Science when you are going to drop it in the spring because you have come down with a case of senioritis. Don't do either of these things: drop a course nor come down with senioritis. **See Chapter 28, Senioritis—finishing strong.**

If you are a high school senior, report that your current year courses are in progress or there is no grade yet. Do not apply weight to your grade nor average your grades together, just report.

Special notes: If you had attended a former high school other than the high school that you currently attend, do not enter the name of your former high school, as the reporting system will get confused and it will appear as though you graduated from two separate high schools, when in fact you are only obtaining a diploma from one high school—the high school that you currently attend. You will report courses and grades from your "old" high school as though you took them at your current school.

If your school gives final grades for a full-year course by each semester, then list the same course twice and enter each final grade across each different term, indicating the final grade for each term received.

If you've taken math or world language in middle school that would otherwise count as a prerequisite to the math and language you had taken at the high school level, please indicate those courses on your SRAR, in the middle school section of the reporting tool.

REFERENCES

SSAR-SRAR. "Self-Reported Student Academic Record." January 8, 2023. https://ssar.selfreportedtranscript.com/Login.aspx.

"Which Colleges/Universities Accept the SRAR?" https://scarletcs.zendesk. com/hc/en-us/articles/360024423094-Which-colleges-universities-accept-the-SRAR©

KEY TAKEAWAYS

SRAR has definitive deadlines. Keep watch.

Accuracy and attention to detail is key.

Keep watch over your email inbox, as often the link to the college's SRAR comes via portal invites from your college, for example, Pennsylvania State University (PSU), Temple University (Temple U portal).

11

ALTERNATIVE BRANCH CAMPUSES AND VARIOUS SEMESTER STARTS (INCLUDING SUMMER)

Some colleges may offer an alternative, less traditional matriculation start via acceptance to an institution's satellite or branch campus location versus their main campus, which, for many, is idealistically slated as their most preferred and sought-after. Imagine due to circumstances of candidacy—perhaps you have not yet fully met the threshold of acceptance criteria, or you were not accepted to the institution's college or program of choice—you could matriculate into the institution through alternative means (alternative campus). This offers you decision flexibility without a closed and shut rejection. Some of you may choose to apply to satellite campuses, heavily suspecting from the start that you may be denied admissions to a university's main campus; whereas others may choose to attend a branch campus due to location proximity, level of academic competition, or comfort level of a smaller campus size. Regardless of the pathway of how you are admitted to a branch campus, you may consider this route a plausible means to attend an institution of your choice. For example, Pennsylvania State University has a multi-campus structure with 24 locations from which to choose. Regardless of campus location, students graduating from the institution do so under the umbrella of Pennsylvania State University as a whole. All degrees earned from this state institution come from PSU without the demarcation of an alternate branch. As you may experience, some will have a greater chance of entrance into a specific major

DOI: 10.4324/9781003380948-13

through the pathway of acceptance to a branch campus for several reasons: availability of enrollment seats, major-specific programming, specialized interests, academic preparedness, and level of competition. Some students may need to demonstrate success by completing 30 credits before transfer.

Some colleges may offer summer starts at leading, most popular campuses which can serve as a wonderful alternative for you to begin matriculation onto any one campus under the umbrella of the main university or college system. The benefits of summer starts are plenty: priority scheduling of general requirements, engage in smaller class sizes, acclimate to campus—engage with peers, early enrollment, make new friends, and adjust to living on campus—before the full return of students for the start of the fall semester.

KEY TAKEAWAYS

Alternative campuses, for example, satellite branches and summer start programs, can offer beneficial aspects to types of applicants for a variety of reasons.

12

THE VALUE OF SPIKED INTEREST VS. WELL-ROUNDED

DEPTH VS. BREADTH

Students are often overwhelmed with the thought of being under-whelming to any admissions committee, when in fact they may be looking at their profiling potential differently. It's easy to feel that you are not doing enough, or that you have not signed up for enough clubs, or maybe you're worried that you're not involved in a sport. Then what? What equates to enough? Let's look at it this way. Instead of thinking breadth and width, think of type of inter-est, level of meaning, and strength of commitment. Think in terms of depth and to what extent—duration and longevity. How long have you been involved in something? To what degree is your calling? How committed are you to this task, sport, item? Colleges want to know how a student is motivated; what drives a student? Demonstrated interests across a saturated list of ten to 20 areas of involvement and representation can be meaningless, whereas a list of one or two life-changing areas of interest and career-like involvement, life's calling perhaps, will impress an admissions rep far greater than an endless list of tasks and associations that were ultimately meaningless for a student on a scale of life-changing and empowering. These so-called spiked interests are those demon-strating growth and continuous dedication over the course of time, for example, dance, gaming, computer hardware gaming kit design, entrepreneurship (self-declared business), self-published author, poet, etc.

DOI: 10.4324/9781003380948-14

WHAT ARE COLLEGES LOOKING FOR?

Colleges are a potpourri of represented strengths, skills, musical talent, voices, athlete, mathematics-minded, research-driven, eclectically diverse populations of people that are drawn from various geographic, socioeconomic, cultural, and academic landscapes that together fill certain populous buckets of any one institution. For a college to achieve its populous fill, it seeks students who have unique and impact-rearing interests–those that were revered on one's application. So, if you are listing "important factors about me" or "extracurricular activities," certainly list your babysitting experience and peer tutoring, but remember to also highlight those interests and activities that truly have shaped your world: karate black belt, marketing and designing for T-shirt company, homemade soaps for homeless shelter, self-created gardening podcast, communal garden, design fundraising initiatives, etc.

One great thing about COVID (if there is one) is the time availed to each of us. Time to be with family and self, time to reinvent the old wheels of static and status quo, time to pivot our thinking and return to what has been a dying pastime—being creative. Many people have capitalized on this newfound availability of time and space to think differently, to act in positive and new ways. As a candidate, ask yourself: how has COVID shaped my thinking and how and where I spend my time?

KEY TAKEAWAYS

Students often worry about not having enough great qualities or involvements for colleges to consider their level of impact as a candidate.

Students are encouraged to delve into extracurriculars that are of special importance to themselves. Think what is of interest to yourself, instead of what looks good.

Colleges will want to know how students invest their time and in what capacities and to what degree. Think quality, not quantity.

Colleges have a campus of diverse strengths, abilities, traits of character, and skill sets.

Campuses often seek students who exhibit spiked interests which can further diversify their campus, and often seek out spiked interests of student applicants to impact and enrich their campus.

PART 3

THE PARTS OF THE APPLICATION

THE ESSAY VS.
PERSONAL STATEMENT

Many students are at an advantage when it comes to showcasing themselves in the form of writing. If given the option, especially over standardized exams, many students are likely to prefer this opportunity to showcase their talents, personality, and character in qualitative writing than rely on standardized exams to demonstrate quantitative measure. Now if you are a student who is reflected poorly through testing and cannot write to save yourself, then I hope you can get by on looks alone. Kidding! Remember, there is a college for everyone. Yours just may take some deep searching to find, and no matter what, each college prioritizes varying types of criteria they are seeking for admissions.

Temple University in Philadelphia, as an example, proposes a test-optional admissions option for students who would rather not submit standardized exam scores due to low scores or an absence of exam scores altogether, but instead will submit various essay components and written responses to prompts. In these incidents, students are not only able to speak of their strengths, but college admissions counselors get an inside look at an applicant's thought process. It showcases creativity, problem-solving, organization, and personality as well as persuasion and convictions—what drives a person? Overall, essay components can showcase one's overall skills and accomplishments.

The essay is a fuller composition in response to an organized and scripted prompt. Common App, for example, currently offers seven prompts from which to choose, one being a free verse allowing for an open dialogue to a self-chosen topic. The word count is up to 650 words and no more, whereas the personal statement is a shorter,

DOI: 10.4324/9781003380948-16

tighter, but freer-versed reply. It is open-ended and usually does not require a specific response to a scripted prompt. It's an opportunity for an applicant to demonstrate wisdom, quirkiness, humor, and even dare to be insightful and indicate a true talent, idiosyncrasy, strange habit, or random skill, for example, having the loudest clap of all. Personal statements are usually between 250–650 words.

 ## KEY TAKEAWAYS

Essays and personal statements can be a great way to showcase talent, niche interest, personality, and unique character traits.

Test-optional colleges often impose essay requirements in lieu of standardized exam scores.

Adhere to word count caps.

14

VALUE OF THE LORS (LETTERS OF RECOMMENDATION)

TEACHER LETTER OF RECOMMENDATION

Most institutions will accept letters of recommendations, but some, usually larger public institutions, will not accept them. Usually, you are guided to submit two letters of recommendation from teachers across two core content areas, for example, English and math or science and literature. Some colleges will require a letter from a specific content teacher such as physics depending on whether a student has applied as an engineering major or perhaps even pre-med. A teacher's letter of recommendation should capture aspects of how you learn as a student, how you think outside the box, or how you generate and lead class discussions; it can even highlight an area of challenge or struggle and indicate how you have overcome and worked through this difficult concept. These letters should not regurgitate the list of student activities or topical details already outside and apparent on the student's application materials such as GPA or supplied resume. Rather, the teacher's letter highlights you, the student, as a learner and leader and how you incorporate and apply knowledge.

COUNSELOR LETTER OF RECOMMENDATION

Parallel to the teacher's letter of recommendation is the counselor's letter. Here, this letter may not be required but may be obtained at the request of the student, and it will complementarily embody the student as a whole person. This letter is less about academics, and it will certainly not detail anything about the student as a learner

DOI: 10.4324/9781003380948-17

within the classroom, as counselors are not teaching the student in this capacity. Rather, a counselor letter can serve as a bird's-eye view of the student in the context to the school as a whole, the interrelatedness of the student among their peers and staff, as well as contributions made by the student to their own learning, career, and college research and planning as well as level of engagement in the processes involved in this overall post-secondary exploration.

THIRD-PARTY LETTER OF RECOMMENDATION

Some students may wish to obtain what I refer to as a third-party letter—one which is authored and submitted to the colleges by one other than a schoolteacher, counselor, or other academically related entity. This person can be a coach, a former teacher from a former high school that the student attended, a supervisor to the student from within an employment or volunteering capacity. These letters can get tricky and often may be unnecessary. I would suggest to students that more is not often better, and in the case of a third-party letter specifically, individual circumstances may warrant such a letter, but again, in most cases they are tertiary and may be ill-regarded as pertinent to an application. One key bit of advice regardless of the type of teacher, the class in which you were taught, and the circumstances and capacities of how a recommender knows the applicant: make sure the recommender is current and can speak to the student in a current manner. It is wonderful that you connected with a teacher in freshman year, but if you had not had another class with that teacher since then, memory recall may not bode well for the applicant, and quite honestly, a lot of growth and maturity takes place between freshman year and senior year of which the teacher may not have experienced or witnessed of the student and, therefore, may not be able to convincingly capture in a letter of recommendation.

WHO TO ASK AND CHOOSE FOR A LETTER?

Many times, the question comes up from students: do I have to ask a teacher for a recommendation from a teacher in whose class I received an A? Quick answer: absolutely not. In fact, there may be a situation in class where a student struggled but persevered and challenged through a struggle only to demonstrate true grit, determination, and resolve and whose grade improvement went from a D to a B. This marked change and response to adversity is a great capture in any letter of recommendation. It shows that a student is real and has real strengths and areas of challenge and they learned how to adapt, take charge of their learning, and persevere.

So make sure recommenders are relevant, relatable, and reflective. Letters overall should forecast and capitalize on person as a learner (hands-on, listener, topic generator), person as leader (peer inspiration, group performer, silent, independent, and passive leader), and person as contributor (where does student struggle and shine?). Content in the letter should capture context: how the recommender knows the applicant, how long and in what capacity, what is striking about the student and different from others, where might the student best learn and contribute to the thought process and learning of others, what type of environment would further one's interest and skills while also fostering new ones, and, last and most important, why this student?

KEY TAKEAWAYS

Students should seek and obtain two letters of recommendation from content teachers.

Colleges will vary on how many letters of recommendations they will allow (usually from one to four).

Some larger data-driven colleges may not accept LORs at all (e.g., Penn State University).

Seek a letter from a teacher that knows you best, not necessarily from a class that you received an easy A.

Occasionally, a student seeks a recommendation from an outside party—a third-party letter—perhaps from a coach, supervisor, or employer. While this is not necessary, sometimes this letter can provide insight on strengths and character that are not reflected in the HS letter.

Seek a LOR well in advance—ask right before junior year ends.

SOCIAL MEDIA AND EMAIL ETIQUETTE

YOUR SOCIAL MEDIA ACCOUNTS—WHO'S REALLY CHECKING?

It should come as no surprise—yet time and time again, it does—that digital footprints are everywhere, and just because one's Instagram caption, YouTube posts, TikTok, Facebook walls, and tweets as well as deleted, ghosted, or abandoned accounts may be inactive, screenshots and clips can resurface at any time. Digital tracing is a thing. Twitter trolls are a thing. In fact, according to the latest Kaplan survey from January 2020,

> The trend across those Admissions officers surveyed from 247 of the nation's top national, regional, and liberal arts colleges and universities—as compiled by U.S. News & World Report—shows an increase in thinking that checking an applicant's social media as fair game—a rise from 57% to 65% from 2019 to 2021. Comparatively, trends from 2019 to 2021 indicate a rise in the percentage of admissions officers finding that what was found has a negative impact on the applicant's outcome, citing a spike from 32% to 58% between 2019 to 2021 data. Commonly, the data suggests that the positive impact to applicants remained steady and unwavering at 38%. Taking the contrarian view, 34% (2022) and 41% (2020) of admissions officers consider viewing applicants' social media "an invasion of privacy that shouldn't be done."

The survey found that 27% of admissions officers visit applicants' social media profiles to learn more about them—significantly down

DOI: 10.4324/9781003380948-18

from 36% in Kaplan's 2020 and 2022 surveys. Overall, college admissions officers are still very much heavily focused on evaluating the fit and appropriateness of a candidate by reviewing the traditional components of the application: GPA, standardized test scores, letters of recommendation, admissions essays, and extracurriculars.

Russell Schaffer (2020). www.kaptest.com/blog/press/2020/01/13/kaplan-survey-percentage-of-college-admissions-officers-who-visit-applicants-social-media-pages-on-the-rise-again/?ranMID=1697&ranEAID=je6NUbpObpQ&ranSiteID=je6NUbpObpQ-ADPOF-dO9mSMFO%2FMr63K1ZA&cmp=aff:linkshare_je6NUbpObpQ)

Russell Schaffer (2022). www.kaptest.com/blog/press/2022/02/01/kaplan-survey-the-percentage-of-college-admissions-officers-who-say-applicants-social-media-content-is-fair-game-ticks-up/

Seventy-one percent of colleges feel that reviewing applicants' social media is fair game. In fact, Harvard University rescinded offers to ten students in 2017 for racist comments (www.insidehighered.com/admissions/article/2020/06/22/colleges-reverse-admissions-offers). Colleges not only want academically prepared students, but they also seek to admit civically appropriate citizens accepting of all communities, affiliations, and orientations (Jaschik, 2020).

SOCIAL MEDIA IS ALSO OUR FRIEND

Of course, social media can also be our friend. It allows us to follow, like, and comment on public discourse while engaging with institutions and affiliates through a common platform. It is more than acceptable—in fact, it's highly encouraged—to follow a college or like a post. This is a method of demonstrated interest **(also see Chapter 6: Data-driven schools vs. holistic).** Colleges will also track and monitor these positive engagements and media footprints.

When we refer to social presence, we also include communication, messaging, and instant messaging platforms such as email, text, instant messenger, tags, and walls. Clean up your Instagram, Facebook, Discord, Snapchat, and TikTok accounts. Remove tasteless and otherwise suggestive posts. Rule of thumb, if it cannot be posted on Grandma's wall for all to see, then take it down. Clean up your email username (bigjammer@gmail.com is only appropriate for a windsurfer, maybe), screen name, handle, and channel name. What you think may be invisible and private can be reposted and shared by those who do have access to your accounts. Just post with conscience and positive intent.

Professionally sounding and appearing email addresses. You may be surprised to see what email addresses are seen across admissions officers' desks while in exchanges with students and parents. Also, check your Google or email profile photo and/or emoji. Some choices may be off-putting or even offensive and, while chosen innocently, may portray a message about you that is negative despite having had no ill intent.

PERSONAL AND PROFESSIONAL EMAIL ACCOUNT

PPE (not personal protective equipment—do you think we're in a pandemic here?) I am referring to a professional personal email. Get one if you do not have one as you will need to maintain a professional account to use for college applications. Since many colleges are self-reporting institutions **(see Chapter 10: Self-reported academic record (SRAR©/SSAR©),** you will need to provide a valid and independently supported email address. It will be to this personal email address that colleges will invite students to join their college's application portal.

This independent email address should be one that can be maintained with ease and one that is checked often. Since many high school student email accounts are set up to receive in-district emails only from identified approved users, we strongly caution students against using their high school email address on applications, Common App, or College Board as these are likely to be blocked by the high school's firewall. You do not want to miss out on emails regarding pertinent deadlines, scholarship opportunities, and, most importantly, a college acceptance!

Overall advice, create a common "college" account—serving as one heavily monitored account to which you provide colleges and use as registration credentials for those sites that you will be spending quite a bit of time: the Common App, College Board, and specific college admissions' entities (.edu), to name a few.

REFERENCES

Scot Jaschik. "Admissions Offers Revoked Over Racists Comments." Inside-HigheredEd.com, June 22, 2020. www.insidehighered.com/admissions/article/2020/06/22/colleges-reverse-admissions-offers

Russell Schaffer. "Kaplan Survey: Percentage of College Admissions Officers Who Visit Applicants' Social Media Pages on the Rise Again: Kaplan Test Prep." Practice Tests, Tutoring & Prep Courses. January 20, 2020. https://www.kaptest.com/blog/press/2020/01/13/kaplan-survey-percentage-of-college-admissions-officers-who-visit-applicants-social-media-pages-on-the-rise-again/.

Russell Schaffer. Kaplan Survey: Percentage of College Admissions Officers Who Say Applicants' Social Media Content is Fair Game' Ticks Up: Kaplan Test Prep." Practice Tests, Tutoring & Prep Courses. February 1, 2022. https://www.kaptest.com/blog/press/2022/02/01/kaplan-survey-the-percentage-of-college-admissions-officers-who-say-applicants-social-media-content-is-fair-game-ticks-up/.

KEY TAKEAWAYS

Create an appropriate email account to which all college-related correspondence can filter.

Clean up, take down, and unfollow tasteless posts and agencies.

Think about first impressions made from your accounts—how do you wish to be perceived?

Obtain a professional and private email address separate from the high school student account email address.

Use this private email address on all college-related materials, applications, and modes of communication.

Check this email account often, as important and timeline information will arrive from various colleges.

16

WHAT SCHOOLS LOOK AT
Major-specific

Engineering, computer science, nursing, financial, and business programs may turn a closer eye towards specific mathematics courses, grades, and scores on math assessments rather than overall grades in English and evidence-based reading and writing components since these programs are propelled through the lens of formulaic math, structural science and/or computational analysis, exact proportions, and/or statistical propositions. A strong foundation for mathematics, as demonstrated by assessment scores, or reflected in grades on transcripts, strongly supports that a candidate is prepared for the higher-level program to which they are applying. Whereas a weaker performance in math may indicate a struggle and, therefore, may negatively impact an admissions decision, or offer admissions with a layer of contingency, which may look like a summer course prerequisite or remedial coursework prior to full matriculation into a program or even academic probation from the start until mastery of concept and content is evidenced.

You can help your case by repeating a core course over the summer at the college level and demonstrate proficiency in this content area through an official college transcript. While your high school may not accept this credit via dual credit or dual enrollment, that is okay, as you will have an official college transcript already in the works. Be careful, however, as this is an official record marking your commencement of coursework at the college level. You'll want to do as best as you can.

Of course, any good college will look beyond your coursework as well and scrutinize areas of key importance: how you've demonstrated collaboration, working in groups, and overall strength of

DOI: 10.4324/9781003380948-19

communication across various modes. After all, many of these STEM majors involve working with others and leading groups. Many aspects are not conducted in isolation, so while your least favorite subject may have been English, and your transcript shows this, you'll want to showcase that you are fully capable of engaging with others efficiently and effectively. These aspects can be showcased through writing samples, such as your essay, and a teacher or counselor letter of recommendation.

KEY TAKEAWAYS

Certain majors may look upon core content classes in more depth to assess level of preparedness for higher-level learning.

17

WORLD LANGUAGE

As a school counselor, I have worked within two very different school systems—one that had a world language graduation requirement of two full years of the same language at the high school level; and the other district that did not have such a graduation requirement. Regardless of whether the credits and experience were tied to one fulfilling requirements and receiving a diploma, I would strongly encourage all students to take at least two full years concurrently of the same world language (i.e., Spanish I and Spanish II) while enrolled in the high school level. This will certainly demonstrate initiative, while almost always fulfill a world language recommendation posted by colleges' admissions criteria. In addition, taking years of a world language can also provide a strong-enough foundation to place out of a college-level language requirement through a competency exam or placement indicator.

Now more selective colleges may highly recommend three or four years of a world language at the high school level, whereas most colleges will require two years. A general rule to consider is that the more years of a language, perhaps the stronger and more attractive the credentials. Balance, however, is key, as well as the opportunity to venture into new and different courses. If adding a third or fourth year of world language prevents you from taking AP® Computer Science or another course offering from a scheduling standpoint, then perhaps taking the new course offers greater benefit, not to mention diversification, higher-level involvement, and places one out of an otherwise comfort zone—all good and defendable reasons to diversify.

DOI: 10.4324/9781003380948-20

KEY TAKEAWAYS

Recommended two years of a language at the high school level.

Balance is key: take higher-level courses or new course offerings in place of WL, to showcase strengths.

Most competitive and highly selective colleges will require three or four years of a language for admissions.

Check college graduation requirements, as most colleges will have a world language requirement.

One could seemingly take a placement exam and be exempted from language, usually with a third level of language at the high school level.

PART 4

AFTER THE APPLICATION

18

YOU'VE BEEN DEFERRED OR WAIT-LISTED. . . . NOW WHAT?

A deferral or wait-list from a college can be upsetting, but on the positive side . . ., you've not been rejected. You have met the criteria that the college is seeking, but in the case of a deferral, the college wants to await receipt of further information on which to make a decision about you; therefore, you have been moved to the regular admissions pool. Whereas, a wait-listed candidate is, for all intents and purposes, in and accepted, but there is yet no available spot in the incoming class. Both scenarios require the candidate to remain patient and optimistic. Both scenarios also offer the following suggestions:

Follow the directions posted from the admissions office as to how to respond and submit additional materials, if requested:

- Submit a security deposit to another school, especially if wait-listed.
- Send in a *new* letter of recommendation.
- Accept your continuance for evaluation for either wait-list or deferral listing—this shows your continued intent on being considered for the college of choice.
- Send a letter or email expressing continued interest. For deferrals, your letter should reflect new information that was not previously sent with your original application and cite data. Examples may include the following:
  - Newer grades/addition of courses
  - Honor or award received
  - Uptick in enrollment % within a school club that you manage
  - Increase in numbers of students utilizing peer tutoring program that you coordinate

DOI: 10.4324/9781003380948-22

Often, deferred candidates will receive a decision before the universal notification deadline of May 1st; however, it is very unlikely that wait-listed candidates will receive a decision prior to May 1st. As a result, it is very important that deferred students act and secure a deposit at a backup college that they have been admitted to no later than May 1st.

 ## KEY TAKEAWAYS

Deferred or wait-listed candidates are still viable candidates for admission.

Students must act depending on the scenario.

Read and follow the instructions from the college on "next steps."

Take recommended actions such as submitting a new letter expressing continued interest, new data-based accolade, honor, or award.

Submit a deposit on a college before 5/1, just in case you are not accepted off the deferral or wait-list.

19

TRANSFERABILITY VS. APPLY DIRECT

Despite all the time, research, planning, academic preparation, and decision-making that goes into selecting the right college, circumstances in life present variables that may impact the road that we are traveling as college students. Sometimes colleges do not offer exactly what the student had hoped for; athletes may get injured and lose scholarship monies, preventing them from continuing at their institution; and other life events change, which may result in a college change as well. Transferring to a new college is not difficult, but it does take some proper planning, paperwork, and deep-to-the-core consideration. It is likely that one may consider transferring within their first year at a college. If this is the case, I am certain the trauma imposed from the original application process getting you into this current college that you are in is still fresh on the brain, and fresh on parents' and guardian's wallets. Choosing and committing to a college is not something that you want to do more than once and certainly not more than twice. Still fresh and not too far in the past, you venture again into the whirly process of obtaining transfer grades, perhaps letters of recommendation, and even financial aid all over again. But, let's face it, if where you are currently is not meeting your needs, hopes, and aspirations, and you cannot see yourself riding out beyond the wave breaks of away-from-home jitters or homesickness and feelings of perpetual aloneness or doom—which can often plague one's first semester away from home and is completely normal—then . . ., well, a deep look at transferring is a must.

DOI: 10.4324/9781003380948-23

REASONS TO TRANSFER

Some reasons to transfer are no-brainers: you've decided to explore mortuary services, and your liberal arts college is not expansive enough and simply does not offer this major, or your baseball team dissolved, and the athletic scholarship that came with it did too. Not far from truth, Wesley College lost its NCAA athletic game rostering when purchased by Delaware State University. For those student-athletes, this may not have been the grand slam that they were looking for (Tresolini, 2021).

We also find that there are deliberate reasons for a transfer from one institution to another. Reasons such as financial sense and time-saving measures are strong considerations for one attending a two-year college under the transfer agreement articulated between community college and in-state (especially) private and public state institutions. The lead examples that I can offer are Massasoit Community College in Massachusetts transfer to UMass system school: UMass Boston, UMass Lowell, UMass Amherst, UMass Dartmouth; or Montgomery County or Bucks County Community College in Pennsylvania transfer to Temple University. It is important for students to ask any community college what kinds of support they provide to assist the candidate with the transfer process. Some questions to ask may pertain to overall campus connections between the two-year college to four-year institution, especially with midyear, semester transfers. What might the candidate need to address from a housing, financial aid, or course selection process? Many of these entities may not carry over seamlessly, and a whole new application process or housing lottery system ensues. Are there guaranteed transfer and admissions requirements of specific programs, for example, nursing or business finance? Does the receiving transfer college have any requisites or graduation requirements such as world language, lab science, etc. that one must complete to meet the transfer requirements set by the receiving college? Does the receiving college coordinate with the sending college so that courses are as best aligned as possible?

Four-year in-state institutions have what we call transfer articulation agreements, and out-of-state institutions may even have what are called reciprocity transfer agreements between out-of-state two-year institutions and four-year institutions; however, the transferability of out-of-state credits is low as out-of-state university systems reserve the right not to accepts any, many, or all transfer credits unless they have been identified as approved courses by their admissions teams. The entry-level, prerequisite courses—versus elective courses often referred to as level 100s—are almost always accepted by all four-year institutions, and they are typically easier to transfer even into out-of-state institutions. It pays to do some research before making any decisions about transferring, so that you can assess risk versus reward in the case of transfer credits. Rule of thumb: if you plan to take courses at an out-of-state school on a temporary basis and then have the credits transferred back to your home institution, check to ensure that the transfer will be permitted before signing up for courses.

Transferring from one college to the next takes careful consideration and should not be taken lightly. There are some unavoidable reasons to consider transferring that extend beyond the academic and aesthetic lens, which may include a loss of scholarship or loss of financial assistance, a family emergency, or a significant change in one's own personal health impacting the ability to sustain; while there are also some situations that play out which, I would caution, should take pause and evolve into a heavier consideration. These are roommate deteriorations, conflicts with friends, and climate and culture differences which may impact your feeling of overall fit. Please know that assimilating on a college campus—away from the comfort and familiarity of home, family, and friends—is not easy. Living with new people and cohabitating with strangers can feel uncomfortable and foreign, yet, having lived through the experience, I urge you to give it some time, at least a semester.

YOU'VE DECIDED TO TRANSFER . . . THINGS TO DO

So, depending on the circumstance, and perhaps one mentioned earlier mirrors your situation, it's inevitable: you've decided to leave your college and finish your education at another institution. Here's how to plan: ask for an official transcript from your current college's bursar or registrar's office, and have it sent to the college to which you wish to transfer. You may need a letter of recommendation from a college advisor or professor, contact the college's financial aid office to inquire about what forms may need to be completed—the college may simply need to be added to the FAFSA® listing, contact admissions office to inquire about what course will transfer in for credit, and, lastly, inquire about housing—on-campus or off-campus, whichever suits your needs. Transferring colleges still has its many layers, including the application and acceptance process—which, as you remember, may not have seemed that long in the past but demands just as much time as the first go-around.

Do your homework and review the transfer application and familiarize yourself with the process. When identifying the right college for transfer, be prepared to articulate *why* and *how* the transfer college is the better fit. Be prepared to recognize the reality often associated with transferring to your new college. Some transfer admission rates are lower or more competitive than the first early action or general admit pool stats. We see this often occurring for the highly competitive institutions, whereas other colleges have higher and more consistent transfer admission rates. Recognize the reality facing the consideration of your transfer application.

Since there are many facets to complete the transfer process from a paper standpoint, get used to learning on friends, colleagues, family, and school resources such as the bursar and advising offices, but be prepared to go this alone, as you will not have a school counselor as you had at the high school level to remind you of deadlines, communicate on your behalf, and, overall, get you to the finish line.

REFERENCE

Kedvin Tresolini. "Sal to DSU Spells End of Wesley College Sports." DelawareOnline.com, February 16, 2021. www.delawareonline.com/story/sports/2021/02/16/sale-delaware-state-spells-end-wesley-college-sports/6759066002/.

 ## KEY TAKEAWAYS

Life happens, and as a result, you may find yourself in a situation contemplating transferring from one college to another.

Some reasons for transfer are to move from a two-year community college to a four-year institution, a transfer from a satellite bridge campus to a main campus of university, loss of scholarship, change in major, being unhappy with current college choice, and life happenstances not-otherwise-specified.

Steps to review before transferring: contact admissions, financial aid, housing offices at prospective college.

There are key questions to have in mind that may put the transfer applicant in the best position for success when planning a transfer between branch campus to main campus or two separate and distinct college systems.

Prepare for records to be sent: official transcript, possible letters of recommendation, and Common App (if using this app) along with the transfer secondary report.

Gain support of family, friends, colleagues, and college-level entities to support your transfer.

APPLYING UNDECIDED—
DEVELOPMENTAL STUDIES

Certain institutions (and the schools and colleges within the larger institution) are more well-known for specific career-preparing programs, or majors such as nursing, engineering, and/or business, and, as a result, these small-niche programs may limit the number of candidates admitted to the program. Ultimately, the competition is greater at these select programs and schools and colleges within the larger institution. Some programs may even carry their own set of applicant credentials: higher GPA requirements, base mathematics standardized exam score, preferential letter of recommendation, and/or separate and distinct application along with a deadline. Why is this worthy of mention? It's simple: as competition increases, your chances of acceptance decrease. Not to fret, as some institutions may allow for you to apply as "undecided" or through their developmental studies program, which is a fancy name given to studies attributed to those who are undeclared; and in some rarer circumstances, while admissions are higher in some colleges within a larger institution such as College of Arts and Sciences, or School of Education, and even College of Liberal Studies, one may transfer within their internal college system once accepted to the main institution, thereby allowing one to enter into the college program of their choice versus the direct admission process. Just to provide a scenario, the University of Iowa indicates on their admissions page (https://admissions.uiowa.edu/academics/first-year-admission-nursing) that they accept 80 students to their nursing school program. Students who ideally meet their direct admission qualifications are considered for direct admission to their nursing program. Students who do not meet their criteria but are indicated as assured

DOI: 10.4324/9781003380948-24

admission, and that that may be wait-listed—having met enrollment criteria but simply are placed on a wait-list—may apply directly (and some are encouraged to do so) to the College of Liberal Arts and Sciences where likely they would indicate specific nursing interest. Students in either case would be reviewed within the standard admissions review cycle. Those that have met the criteria and who wish to be reviewed for direct admissions to the nursing program would otherwise apply directly to the College of Nursing.

It is worth noting that due to the high level of competition and smaller enrollment sizes of key programs such as nursing and engineering, most students will apply directly to specific colleges within the larger institution programs. Direct admission programs are fiercely competitive and often do not offer sideways enrollment options like assured admission or even transferability into such a program outside of original, direct, and initial matriculation from the very start of first year enrollment on campus. Colleges such as University of Florida and Pennsylvania State University offer direct admissions or early admit enrollments in their nursing programs. Students are unable to transfer into nursing from other programs or other satellite campuses or other colleges once the freshman year is underway.

Despite there being various avenues for applying, it cannot be emphasized enough that there are no guarantees. Trickery may exist in the minds of some candidates and their families in thinking they may be gaming the system, that is, applying for general studies or science undeclared but having all intents and purposes of pursuing a degree in nursing or physical therapy. You get my point. Top-select programs and those that are highly competitive by nature—medical, architecture, engineering, finance, business—are limited and rule-bound. Even the top puzzle-doer may not be able to break the admissions code.

There have been situations where students have changed intended majors after applying, with the hopes of gaining acceptance at a more desirable campus of an institution, or they have opted for summer starts, which was discussed in greater detail in **Chapter 11, Alternative branch campuses and various semester starts.** While neither of these options guarantees acceptance, it can provide access to an alternate method for review. Note to applicant: listing an alternate major (one that you do not intend pursuing) or declaring as undecided when you know what major you are wanting to pursue can be counterproductive, and once admitted, there is no guarantee that you can switch majors or declare in an impacted field, as things get tricky. Competitive and select majors have different review criteria and processes; and sometimes being considered for your truly intended major is like cutting through strict bureaucracy. Plus, college admissions committees catch on. Also, many nursing and engineering programs are *direct admission*, meaning that one must declare at the time of applying. There is no wiggle room in these incidents to transfer into one's program of choice at a later date.

Different schools versus different majors also adds to the complexity and difficulty of trying to rig the system. For those that wish to change majors within the same discipline, usually no worries. However, if your newly intended major is listed within a college or institution different from your new major, then you are subject to a different review committee, requirements, and standards. For example, applying for criminal justice or sociology may not pose an issue because both majors are likely housed in the College of Arts and Sciences; yet engineering and finance will be in two separate schools within a larger institution.

REFERENCE

https://admissions.uiowa.edu/academics/first-year-admission-nursing

 KEY TAKEAWAYS

Applying to competitive programs may require one to disclose their major up front.

Some students may be assumed as admitted to a program through assured admission. They will need to apply to a liberal arts program with the hope of eventually transferring into their specific program.

Most direct admit programs do not offer the flexibility of transferring into a desired program after matriculation into the college.

21

ROTC AND SERVICE ACADEMY CANDIDATES

ROTC PROGRAMS

Reserve Officers Training Corps (ROTC) programs are offered at plenty of colleges and universities outfitted to train candidates as committed military reservists. While the Navy, Army, and Air Force each has its own ROTC program, the Marines do not, yet one interested in becoming a Marines can do so through the Marine option through the Navy. The Coast Guard also has a pre-candidate training program offering skills training and scholarship opportunities.

SERVICE ACADEMIES

While both ROTC programs (offered at civilian schools) and Service Academy training are both set to graduate commissioned officer's rank and bachelor's degrees, there are some significant differences to consider. Student applicants should ask themselves whether they want to have a traditional college experience with respect to social life, campus involvement, recreational freedom, quad living, or fraternity involvement as well as off-campus liberties such as off-campus living, socializing etc. Service Academies come with a very structured lifestyle including scheduled workouts and mealtimes, commitment to uniform, dress code, curfews, mandatory participation in varsity sports, and attendance at school-wide sporting events, to name a few. Service Academy requirements also involve a highly selective academic rigor and arduous upkeep of academic performance across the years. Truly, academics are the fabric of the service academy webbing. All students must graduate within five years.

DOI: 10.4324/9781003380948-25

Students otherwise interested in ROTC programming within a university would be assumed to attend training three to five times per year, with a rotation of on-and-off weekends. While uniforms are also worn, there are many days and events at which ROTC candidates can wear civilian clothing.

One major importance to note is the application process for Service Academies is lengthy and begins well before the senior year, during which most of all applications are completed. In fact, the multilayers of the application begin in one's junior year. The following components make up the application process to Service Academies:

☐ Academic preparedness
☐ Letter of nomination from a State Senator or House of Representatives
☐ Physical fitness
☐ Optional: Junior year offerings: summer Junior Cadet School (Army) or Summer Seminar (Air Force, Navy) pre-acceptance programs
☐ SAT or ACT score
☐ Pass a medical exam
☐ Demonstrated leadership

If you are at all contemplating attending a Service Academy or participating in an ROTC program, it is important to speak with your school counselor as soon as possible so they can best guide you through the process.

 ## KEY TAKEAWAYS

ROTC and Service Academy programming offers unique and structured programming to confirm commission-ranked branch candidates.

ROTC programming offers flexibility across majors and academics.

Service Academy enrollment strictly adheres to tight academic pathways and offers less of a traditional college experience, including campus liberties.

Major differences exist among programming, traditional college aspects, and cadet requirements.

Service Academy application process begins early—junior year—and has many layers.

22

ATHLETES AND ATHLETIC DIVISION I/II AND III CONSIDERATIONS AND RECRUITMENT

STUDENT-ATHLETE: WHAT TO EXPECT

Deciding on whether to play a sport at the college level takes some serious consideration as the timeliness and layering of application components will precede and parallel those of the official application process. Divisional play (DI/DII and even DIII) takes not only a serious commitment but can also dictate the type of experience one will have at the college. DI and DII participation involves organized meals, practices (sometimes two a day) on-season and off-season training regiments, curfews, and even on-the-road tutoring to offset missing classes due to game schedules; these are some of the programmed expectations of participating at the top divisional athletic levels. Of course, there are also many perks as well such as free workout clothing, grab-and-go nutritional snacks, full on-the-road meals, academic supports, and personalized tutors, as well as student-athlete housing and course selection priority, to name a few.

NATIONAL COLLEGIATE ATHLETICS ASSOCIATION (NCAA)

During one's junior year, a student applicant is highly recommended to register with the National Collegiate Athletics Association (NCAA)—a clearinghouse of all academic eligibility and information listed about rules and regulations associated with athletic academic requirements for both Divisions I and II eligibility and recruitment

DOI: 10.4324/9781003380948-26

processes—when can coaches contact you? NCAA Eligibility Center: https://web3.ncaa.org/ecwr3/.

I highly recommend all junior athlete-potentials register with the NCAA Clearinghouse and review the academic requirements for the upper divisions of collegiate participation and eligibility. For example, DI colleges require 16 academic course credits across English, social studies, math, social science, and science content areas, whereas DII requires 14 academic credits. Speak with your high school's NCAA coordinator to confirm which high school courses are approved by the NCAA, as each high school is required to submit a course catalog for approval by the clearinghouse to meet eligibility guidelines. Please caution that some academic or foundation level courses may not meet the eligibility requirements of either DI or DII participation.

Secondly, it is highly suggested that students add the NCAA (college code: 9999) to Naviance's *Colleges I am Applying to* list or Scoir's *My Colleges list*, as an entity to receive high school–based application documents such as official transcript, school profile, and other high school–based records that one's counselor will submit to colleges/ entities upon student's request. After all, the NCAA will require an official high school transcript but, new for 2024, will no longer require SAT/ACT scores. Note to students, treat the NCAA as one of your esteemed colleges.

RECRUITMENT AND CONNECTING WITH COACHES

The NCAA is also very specific on recruitment and coach-to-student communications. While most coach-led outreach and direct communications can occur during one's junior year, there are certain sports which allow for communications that begin during the high school sophomore year. Of course, specific allowances will differ across not only the type of sport but also across DI and DII, as well as men's and women's sports. The simplest overview states that coaches representing all sports can reach out directly by phone or email to students in one's junior year, while the exact month allowance may differ slightly across the cast of sports. The best bet is to use caution when communicating with a coach. For specific details of which sports and levels can communicate with student-athlete prospects and when, google the NCAA eligibility center or visit: www.ncsasports.org/ncaa-eligibility-center/recruiting-rules.

Division I football, gymnastics, and wrestling coaches can communicate directly with students specifically about recruitment during a prospective athlete's sophomore year, whereas Division II softball, baseball, football, lacrosse, field hockey, and other coaches can only direct contact in one's junior year. All coaches can send indirect, non-recruitment marketing materials in the form of surveys, brochures, and college non-athletics institutional guides at any time. Serious and structured recruiting contact begins either after June 15 sophomore year or September 1 during one's junior year and will depend on the sport and division level, as referenced earlier.

As with every dreamy vision of being the athletic star comes a counselor's lesson for all cautionary tales. Coaches do make everything sound so wonderful. After all, doesn't everyone want to feel accepted and desired? I only state to use caution when in discussions with a coach. They may be assuring you of a spot on the team, but please know that their decision alone cannot and will not be a shoo-in within the institution, as a student-athlete must, first and foremost, meet the academic requirements of the college or university. This is paramount of all review processes for admissions at an institution prior to athletic acceptance.

REFERENCE

NCAA Eligibility Center. https://web3.ncaa.org/ecwr3/

KEY TAKEAWAYS

There are perks and dedication expectations for student-athletes who wish to play at the collegiate divisional levels.

Student-athletes must meet academic requirements of the institution and are applicants, first and foremost.

Coaches can send non-recruitment materials to prospective student-athletes and can contact athlete prospects as early as sophomore year, depending on the sport and divisional level.

Students who are contemplating playing sports at the collegiate level are highly encouraged to register with the NCAA clearinghouse and add the NCAA to their colleges list in Naviance or Scoir.

PAYING FOR COLLEGE

FEDERAL FUNDS

Federally funded aid can cover expenses such as books, tuition, room and board, living expenses such as food, a personal computer, transportation, and even dependent care, if qualified. The main sources of federal monies come in the form of grants, scholarships, and loans—the former two offer monies that are free and do not need to be paid back, whereas the latter must be paid and often with variable interest incurred.

FAFSA

Applying for federal aid is tedious but relatively easy and completely essential. Apply for federal student aid—grants, loans, scholarships—using the free application for federal student aid (FAFSA®). And remember, the first F in "FAFSA" stands for "free"—you shouldn't pay to fill out the FAFSA form! The FAFSA form you fill out should correspond with the school year you're planning to seek aid for (the year in which you are matriculating in college). For example, if you're applying to college for the 2024 admissions, then you will complete the 2024–2025 FAFSA form.

FAFSA® is the main (of two) application utilized in the determination of family needs and identified expected level of financial contribution towards college expenses, tuition, and fees (Federal Student Aid). The FAFSA® is a government tool that determines the identification of types of federal funds to offset the payment of college based on need. The FAFSA® utilizes family-reported household income among other entities such as 529 plans, retirement plans,

DOI: 10.4324/9781003380948-27

savings accounts, etc. to determine the family's estimated family contribution or EFC. This numerical factor determines how much the family is expected to pay towards the full amount of college attendance.

Colleges will provide families with a financial aid package listing the total cost of attendance, minus the families' estimated contribution (EFC) equaling the remaining financial need which will then be itemized through a variety of listings to include federal grants, scholarships, federal work-study jobs, and a variety of parent and student loans.

CSS PROFILE

The other tool only used by private colleges and universities is called the CSS Profile®, offered by College Board. (CSS Profile. The College Board. https://cssprofile.collegeboard.org/). The profile determines the level of need offset by large institution-based monies (usually sourced by large endowments). Unlike the FAFSA®, the CSS Profile® is not a federal form, and monies coming forth from the calculation of the Profile originate from institution-based sources outside that of the Federal government. When comparing the CSS Profile® against the FAFSA®, two components are true: its factorization takes into account other elements that the FAFSA® does not, such as debt and ownership of property and vehicles—boats included; the CSS Profile® is also not free. The profile, which is by these institutions, carries a cost through College Board and usually runs about $25 for the initial submission to college number one, and somewhere near $16 for each sequential private college or university submittal.

FAFSA AND CSS PROFILE CONSIDERATIONS

Ultimately, these two forms are stand-alone vehicles through which the federal government determines a family's financial aid eligibility. This determination is calculated through a mathematical formula considering income in the household (through all reportable forms): "salary," including alimony and child support payments in cases of divorce. It is important to distinguish that household income refers to those monies that are coming into the household within which the student resides for the majority of the time. The household income of the other parent or guardian with whom the student does not reside or does not reside for the majority of the school year is listed but is not factored into an equation. Rather, this custodial guardian is not the bearer of the FAFSA® completion process at all. Across each of the two financial application platforms, certain varying factors are taken into consideration to determine the magic financial need numbers. These are income, assets, debt, and investment entities such as 401(k), IRA, 403b, 529 plans, annuities, etc. While one can certainly get into the weeds with the ins and outs of these applications, there might be more of a trick to fielding monies into certain quadrants to avoid a penalty for dutiful, aggressive, and planned savings, and a financial planner may be just the person to help guide the anxious check writer of the household before it's time to send in first-semester payments.

Notes worthy of mention: the FAFSA® completion is assumed as required if the student wishes at all to receive or be considered for monetary aid in the form of federal loans and/or federal subsidies and plans such as Work-Study. It is also questionable whether students will be considered eligible for any merit-based monies (academic and talent-based) such as scholarships and grants if they do not complete the FAFSA®. Many colleges and universities differ on this requirement, but it sure would be a loss if one did not complete the forms and missed out on available money. So rule of thumb: take the time to complete these financial aid forms. Also, remember that the first "F" in FAFSA® stands for *free*. Do not get tripped up on a Google search to the wrong financial aid site and succumb to a charge for form completion. The FAFSA® is free. Lastly, first come, first served is the rule of the day. While one should not rush through this process of completing the FAFSA®, one should not wait wherever possible either. The FAFSA® is first available for online access and completion on 10/1.* Colleges will post a priority completion deadline of February 1st or March 15th. I cannot urge you enough to not only meet these dates but precede them, as once monies are allocated to families and students of need and merit, they are gone. The federal government will only allot so much per year, and once allocated, it's gone. DO NOT WAIT. Super lastly, the FAFSA® can list up to ten institutions at one time to receive the application. If one is

---

* Due to Federal government updates, the release of the 2024-25 FAFSA will be 12/1.

applying to more than ten colleges, it is advised to submit the form and await a confirmation email; then return to the form, delete as many colleges from the list as there are additional colleges, and then add the new additions to the list; resubmit and be done.

A little hidden secret here as well: if, when your student receives their financial aid package and letter, you suffer a mini heart attack at the sticker price, your brain spins inside your skull, your hands are sweaty, and you start to hyperventilate, find comfort in knowing that you are not alone; and secondly, once you have regained composure, realize that you can contact the Financial Aid Office at your student's preferred college to inquire about additional monies and/or refactoring the financial aid breakdown. Perhaps a college can award on-campus work-study and reduce the loan structure that is listed, or, based on newer grades, the merit-based scholarship monies may increase, etc. It's always worth the conversation. I'll leave you with some sound advice from my mom: "You'll never know unless you try" and "What's the worst thing that can happen? They say no."

GRANTS

A grant is a form of financial aid that doesn't need to be repaid, unless the basis for the granting of the monies is contingent upon a service or completion expectation such as grade performance, academic enrollment, or employment outcome; for example, the TEACH Grant requires one to become a certified employed teacher.

SCHOLARSHIPS

Free monies derived from local, national, community, school, large corporations such as Dunkin Donuts, Hallmark, Coca-Cola, Microsoft, or an entity in which one has affiliation or membership such as American Legion, Elks club, including a variety of employee-based opportunities. These monies can be renewable or a one-time award usually based on merit, skill, interest, or small niche market.

LOANS

Loans are not gifted, but rather taken out from a financial brokerage firm or entity by a loanee or borrower. Loans are most granted through banking institutions such as banks, online lenders, credit unions, and even credit cards. Each offers a variety of payback, borrowing amount, and interest terms and agreements.

UNSUBSIDIZED VS. SUBSIDIZED

Pertains to loans made to parents or students once federal, state, and local financial aid has been determined. Unsubsidized loans are available to both undergraduate and graduate students with or without financial need. These structured loans accrue interest at the time of disbursement. The government does not offset the payment of these loans, and, with higher loan ceilings, one can easily get into a risky payback situation. Subsidized loans offer undergraduate students interest-held monies based on need that can offset costs. Loan amounts are lower, but paybacks are interest-free until graduation, which likely is an attractive choice for students.

Direct PLUS/Parent PLUS—lower fees and lower interest rates; non-credit based, meaning one's parent's credit status is not a prohibitive or determining factor for the issuance of Direct PLUS loan. Loan fees or "load fees" are significantly less than those of a Parent PLUS loan.

Pro	Con
Fixed interest rate	Incurs interest
Tax-deductible interest	May be apt to borrow too much
Flexible repayment options	Credit check is required
Payback cycle begins immediately upon graduation	
Large origination or "load" fees	

PRIVATE ENTITIES

Parents and students can shop around for the best loan option. Key items to think about and consider are loan amount needed, loan amount available, payment cycle obligation, fixed or variable interest rate, consolidation options, early payment benefits, or payment forgiveness.

WORK-STUDY

Other types of specialized scholarships include but are not limited to Work-Study, which is a federal employment stipend paid directly to full-time enrolled students who hold campus-related positions across various campus departments and entities such as athletics, cafeteria, the business office, admissions, and/or bursar's offices, etc. Monies go directly to the student and not towards tuition directly; therefore, students may choose where and how to spend this money, although the expectation is for the monies from employment to be used to offset college-related expenses versus supplement as income.

MILITARY SCHOLARSHIPS

A vastly alternative method of paying for college; yet the ROTC scholarships pay for full tuition costs, books, room, and board for each of the four years, plus a monthly stipend for living and personal expenses.

Larger benefits include Split Training Option (STO) for the extremely dedicated military cadet who feels that perhaps a career in one of the armed forces branches is destiny. Cadets in this case, with the permission of a parent/guardian, enlist as a junior in high school—age 17—and complete basic combat training over the course of two summers and some weekend commitments prior to even graduating high school and applying to college and university ROTC programs. This opens the doors for many students as they start their career while earning credit towards military branch promotion, training in their field and branch of interest, academic credit benefits for college, as well as money for living.

One of the biggest benefits of an STO is that students can gain leverage and rank quickly, often rolling right into an Advanced Individual Training (AIT) while also enrolling at out-of-state college ROTC programs often for the cost of an in-state student. It's important to note as well that, despite there being a common ROTC scholarship and application process, each branch holds its own unique total year commitment tallies. Most ROTC programs require five, whereas more specialized training such as flight combat training may require eight. It's important to investigate the differences between branches and reservists versus active enlistees.

Little gems are tucked away in the myriad of military scholarships.

REFERENCE

Federal Student Aid. "An Office of the US Department of Education." FAFSA.
https://studentaid.gov/h/apply-for-aid/fafsa

 KEY TAKEAWAYS

- The FAFSA® and CSS Profile® are identified as two financial aid documents used to determine monies awarded to students based on a variety of factors.
- FAFSA® is a free federal form used to determine monies in the form of grants, scholarships, and federal loans.
- EFC—estimated family contribution—is used in part of the FAFSA® 's calculation to identify a portion of attendance costs assumed by families.
- CSS Profile® is a College Board form used at cost to determine institution-based monies towards the costs of attendance.
- CSS Profile® considers a variety of family financial information such as assets and debt which vary from that of the FAFSA®.
- The FAFSA® is assumed a required document as without it, students are not considered for school-based scholarships and other forms of monies.
- Federal funds available through the FAFSA determinations include grants, scholarships, Work-Study, and loans.
- Private monies may arrive in the form of community, affiliation, school, and/or organizations with scholarship and granting agencies.
- Loans can either be unsubsidized or subsidized, yet both offer students and parents options to offset costs associated with attending college, paying living expenses, supplies, dependent care, and other entities related to living on or off campus. Loans come in a variety.
- Military and ROTC scholarships often coincide with some digging into the ROTC and branch websites.
- Benefits include early-commitment STO programs in high school, paychecks, medical and dental coverage, stipends, four-year tuition coverage, books, and room and board.
- Various year commitment tallies vary across the various branches.

ACCUPLACER®/ALEKS®
PLACEMENT EXAMS

All students entering college will take a placement exam in the content areas of mathematics and English. Score results of each will determine which course and course level is recommended for the matriculating freshman student. It goes without saying that stronger performance at high school in both content areas as well as number of courses taken in these content areas will likely indicate a higher placement for the student; or in the case of a world language, perhaps even a waiver of exemption of the requirement fulfillment **(see Chapter 17: World language).**

In some incidences, students may place into a remediation-level English and/or math course prior to entering a credit-bearing requisite course. These courses will always cost money for enrollment, and they are required as they will serve as the foundation for any future course required towards the fulfillment of graduation requirements.

KEY TAKEAWAYS

All first-year students will take an English and math placement exam to indicate the appropriate level of placement.

In some cases, students may be identified as needing an at-cost, non-credit-bearing remediation course prior to enrollment in a creditable requisite course.

DOI: 10.4324/9781003380948-28

25

"THANK YOU"

The power of a great attitude = gratitude

Students, there is no denying that the college application process brings out the best or the worst in each of us. You will have accomplished by the fall of your senior year what had seemed insurmountable back in the spring of your junior year. You have made lists, conducted research, contemplated campuses, negotiated deadlines, visited campuses, written upwards of ten essays, submitted letters of recommendation for a lot of attention, all the while maintaining grades, devotion to campus activities, friends, and family. Those that love you have also devoted their time, compassion, recognition, editing, and proofreading skills; high-fived you and were happy for you when you secured your college wins; and were crushed for you when the rejections came in. Teachers and counselors rooted for you, helped guide you, and were overall in your corner since day one. Now is the time to take pause, breathe, and begin to extend your gratitude for all those who stood with you, by you, in support of you, and those that believed at this moment when you became an almost high school graduate, with your newfound college admittance. Your greatest accomplishments are yet to come, but some of the most remarkable have earned you a spot at the table of college. Congratulations college-bound friend. Continue your greatness. Be humble and hungry, and, above all, remain conscientious, curious, grateful, and wise.

 KEY TAKEAWAYS

Undeniably, you have worked hard to get here. Equally, so have parents/ guardians and all those that have supported you along the way. Continue to be mindful, conscientious, curious, and wise.

DOI: 10.4324/9781003380948-29

PART 5

AFTER ACCEPTANCE

26

MENTAL HEALTH AND BALANCE

Back at the introduction is where mental health first came into the picture. It is repeated here because I think it is very important. Students have internalized so much peer pressure for reasons, likely, that they may have idealized an intangible and unrealistic perfectionism, while also assuming that the name of a college equates to not only success in life but the meaning of oneself. In many ways, the college process and the going-to-college fantasy have forecast a generation of students who prefer outcome versus process. I want so much to hold on to this and attempt to procure a generation of college applicants who see value in the process and who embrace the notion that college is what you make it. If we send students to college who are unfit for independent life, those that may not be able to navigate living alone among strangers, struggling enough to rely on self-assuredness, to access that which is unfamiliar and, in many cases, that which is uncomfortable, and those that must fail—as some of you will falter and stumble, but there are also those who bounce back and rise among all that is *college*—then we must reevaluate *where* and *what* is the best post-secondary experience for you as a student.

College can and should be an option for all that desire it. The when, where, and how may look different for every candidate. Knowing oneself and honestly asking the difficult questions relating to one's own level of preparedness is key. Having the ability to identify the need for help and having the confidence to take advantage of the many on-campus counseling and student support services is crucial to one's success on campus. Students, giving yourself the allowance to not have it all figured out all the time is okay. You're

DOI: 10.4324/9781003380948-31

no longer just learning how to perform in school, but you are learning how to navigate the many complexities of life as an individual adult, in an academic setting where the everyday decisions are no longer guided by external forces or expectations, but instead the pulses and driving forces from within. It's a lot to manage, and there are times when we all need to reach out and get support.

We are proud of you as a student, a learner, a navigator, and a spirit, and we rely on your generation and other generations to follow. Do well and be fulfilled.

 ## KEY TAKEAWAYS

Maintain perspective and balance among elements in one's life.
College admission is a process, but so too is attending college.
Try to shed unrealistic perceptions, goals, and expectations.
College is what you make it—your experience.
Be kind to yourself, patient, humble, and give gratitude.

27

DISABILITIES: SSD AND SDI

Every college is outfitted with a learning center or academic center offering services for ALL students regardless of need. All colleges also have a support center for students with unique or complex learning and thinking differences. Students with differing abilities who have been serviced with an Individualized Educational Plan (IEP) or 504 plan (medical-based) in high school can seek similar accommodations (but not modifications) at the college level. While high schools are obligated to remove barriers to education and ensure academic success while also identifying students in need of services, colleges are obligated to ensure access to academics, but, unlike high schools, they are not obligated to provide modifications to curriculum (e.g., reducing answer choices, reducing problem sets or assessment questions, using word banks, or altering format of exams), nor are they obligated to identify students in need of services. The world of identifying and providing support changes once a student steps out of high school and into the college environment starts with the admissions stage.

As a student, you have your own story to share through the admission process, yet at no time *must* you disclose a disability to the admissions offices, unless this were part of one's personal statement or essay **(please see "The essay vs. personal statement," Chapter 13, for more detail).** Application review committees are not privy to knowledge of a student's disability unless otherwise disclosed through the application materials by the student.

In fact, it is after you have been accepted to the institution that you will make an appointment with the Services for Students with

DOI: 10.4324/9781003380948-32

Disabilities (SSD) office to disclose former IEP- and 504-related plans detailing accommodations and/or modifications. While colleges and universities do not have IEPs or 504 plans, and they are not obligated to provide specialized instruction mirroring that received at the high school level, they are obligated to provide accommodations for those that can provide evidence of a learning disability necessitating the use of accommodations. Overall, colleges are very amenable to providing the means.

What is very important to note: you must take the full reins as a newly accepted college student and register with the college's SSD office (or similar acronym referring to the college's disability services office). You will need to register as *a student with a disability in need of services* and apply for the types of accommodations that were useful in high school. The registration process takes place at the office for students with disabilities and not the college's admissions office.

Many times, students will have extended time on assessments, extended deadlines for assignments, and even a scribe. Some students will show colleges their evaluations used to determine their disabilities as well as a copy of the IEP's SDI page (specifically designed instruction) which outlines the accommodations and modifications received, while others may provide a copy of the high school 504 plan. Rules on proof of evidence are changing at the college level, yet most colleges are seeking current evidence of evaluation (past three years), but check with your college's support office as each institution will work differently.

SOME KEY DIFFERENCES AT THE COLLEGE LEVEL

There are no case managers. Students, brace yourselves. You are revered as an adult as seen in the eyes of the colleges. If you are a student approved for accommodations at the college level, you will no longer receive progress monitoring updates. There is no case manager articulating a plan to you or the college, and there are no annual reviews or team meetings. In fact, the disabilities support officer at some colleges may email a student's accommodations to the faculty; others may bestow this burden of notification onto you, the student.

SOME TYPICAL COLLEGE-LEVEL ACCOMMODATIONS

☐ Use of notetakers for class lectures, or copies of professor's notes
☐ Making audio recordings of lectures
☐ Testing: readers and scribes, taking exams in a smaller quieter location to reduce distraction
☐ Extra set of textbooks

All evaluations at the college level must be conducted independently from the college. Unlike high schools which provide free psycho-educational evaluations and triennial reevaluations (every three years), colleges are not obligated to conduct such testing.

KEY TAKEAWAYS

Accommodations (not modifications) can be made at the college level. Support services will vary from college to college.

The discussion of the need for accommodations comes after a student has been accepted. The student applicant must register with the college's Disabilities Office.

Parents are no longer in the loop. Students must self-advocate and identify need for support.

Students may have to notify professors of disability needs, whereas some college's disabilities officers will notify faculty on behalf of students.

28

SENIORITIS—FINISHING STRONG

Senioritis is not so much a medical term as it is a common term used to describe the nonviral affliction of passiveness, complacency, and downright stopping-in-your-tracks ceasing of any upward momentum in grades, and work completion. It is often associated with presentations consistent with not showing up for class, oversleeping, lack of motivation, less to no studying, and even, yes, we've seen it—the occasional course failure. Don't be this senior. Finish strong. Take advice from the high school coach that told to you to run straight through the finish line; don't slow down to meet it. Seriously, though, colleges are going to celebrate with you at the end when your final transcripts are sent. They, like you, want to make sure that the right fit has been determined and that your success at their institution is highly plausible. If a college finds that you've slacked, and you have not lived up to your potential as your early transcripts once indicated, then they can and likely will rescind their offer of acceptance. Now grades may slip here and there, yes, but you do not want to do a total crash and burn. One of two things can occur. One, indeed, colleges can take back their offer of acceptance or, two, place you on the academic probation list, meaning that you're already on warning of failing out of college without even having started. The implications of academic warning or probation can trickle over to athletics as a redshirted athlete, meaning, due to probation, you are not eligible to participate in collegiate games, matches, or otherwise organized DI, DII, or DIII cross-collegiate competition. Where the impact is felt the hardest may be in the areas of finances, especially if you are an athletic scholarship recipient or

DOI: 10.4324/9781003380948-33

grant recipient who needs to maintain a certain grade percentage or eligibility status confirmed by grade performance.

The overarching theme here for all seniors: celebrate your victories, but also know that your main job is still not over. Celebration at the end of your senior year will be much more glorious knowing you've given all that you could to get there. Finish strong, earn that high school diploma, and make yourself proud. Some ideas to ward off senioritis: reward yourself by celebrating the small success. Perhaps the completion of a final project or an oral presentation. Set goals for yourself, get organized and stick to the task, get an organizer or a calendar, and plot out the remaining weeks of high school and assignment due dates while scheduling breaks and self-care opportunities. Surround yourself with support and those that can help to motivate you. Take a break and be kind to yourself. You've accomplished what once appeared as the most unsurmountable feat—applying and getting accepted to college. Remember what you are working towards and hoping to achieve in the longer run. Make this part of that achievement.

KEY TAKEAWAYS

Senioritis is real. It is not a virus but an affliction of procrastination and lack of work production impacting year-end grades and overall performance which may incur a negative impact on one's college acceptance.

Stay sharp and engaged in your studies, and finish strong.

Strategies to help get to the finish line: stay organized—get a calendar, identify your supports, seek guidance, be kind to yourself, schedule breaks, set realistic goals, celebrate mini milestones and smaller successes along the way, keep your eyes on the prize.

29

PREPARING FOR SUCCESSFUL ARRIVAL ON CAMPUS

As a counselor, I have long contemplated the realization that while much time is spent on preparing, researching, and completing the fibrous applications with their spindly components, not nearly as much time is designated to counseling students on how to prepare for success on the college campus and the nuances of what college life may look like.

There are many nuances that differentiate the academics on a college campus from those at the secondary level. I have stated many subsequently as an overview for students to consider. There could be a book just about the going-to-college experience and navigating the college campus, but, for the purposes of this college application guide, I wanted to explore the items yet not detract from the purposes of the main contents relating to the research and the application process.

Some of the most drastic differences span across academic, social, and personal domains. Many of the anticipated, expected changes relate to social context: living with a roommate and navigating the social scenes, adjusting to life independently and without the structure of home and family, living away for the first time, etc., while some of the more unexpected changes that occur are related to the academic structure. High school students spend roughly 32.5 to 35 hours per week in the classroom, whereas college students will be engaged in 12 to 15.5 hours per week, leaving a plentitude of downtime within the academic week, not to mention the weekend. Time management and the skills surrounding the use of time and unstructured time are critical for survival not only in the academic performance sense but in the social sense as well. Please refer to the subsequent chart outlining the various elements that encompass both the high school and college landscapes but contain vast differences across these two landscapes within three main types of domains: academic, social, and personal.

DOI: 10.4324/9781003380948-34

SUCCESS ON THE COLLEGE CAMPUS

Area of impact	High school	College
Academic Social Personal	Time management: 32.5–35 hours academics/week	Time management: 12–15 hours academics/week
	Full year and semester system (four terms/quarters, two semesters); full year: 36 weeks long	Full semester system (two main terms: fall and spring, some summer sessions I/II); each semester: 15 weeks long
	Teachers present and deliver notes and cover most material in class	Professor lectures, notes written by students, majority of course materials covered outside of class
	School counselor	Academic advisor
	Teachers—after class, prep periods	Professor—office hours/appointments
	Deadlines, extreme circumstance tend to be flexible	Deadlines are no longer suggestions, firm
	Late and overdue = loss of points	Late and overdue = a zero for you
	Class size: up to 35	Class size: 20–100+ depending on institution
	Place to study: room, living room, kitchen table, high school library	Place to study: others to adjust to, may not be own room but library, need to be conscientious of roommate
	Maintain grades: teachers and counselors are most apt to check in with you; periodic reporting: goes home to guardian(s)/parent(s)	Maintain grades: self-motivated, self-monitoring; no one will be checking in on you and asking why you did not attend class
	Attendance taken daily	Attendance often not taken
	Built-in/flexible grade boosts: extra credit, project-based component, redo, or test takeover, curved grades. High schools are more apt to offer flexible credit and grade options such as online credit recovery, correspondence courses, and other "creative," more liberal means to achieve credit	Grades and assignments deadlines are inflexible, no redos or test takeovers, some professors do not assign grades on a curve scale; most majors *require* specific grade cutoffs much higher than typical "passing" score to continue in programming
	Fewer and infrequent long-range curriculum components; more pop-up quizzes and intermittent changes to curriculum based on classroom-based situations and circumstances	Syllabus/course outline of all components, % of grade, due dates and forecast of long-term assignments; structure and flow of content delivery is more rigid and less flexible as all described course content must be covered
	Be prepared to be challenged	Be prepared to be overwhelmed at first; adjustment takes time
	Be prepared to be challenged; seek balance	

(Continued)

Area of impact	High school	College
	Navigating established peer groups	Entering new context; forging new relationships
	Common areas/no ownership of space; accessible by all	Shared living with roommate(s); sense of ownership of space
	Weekly interaction in for set hours/day with general population—full school Heterogeneous mix	Shared housing or residential or Living Learning Communities (LLCs) based on common majors (e.g., Nursing/Engineering)
	Familiar setting; can return home at the end of the day	Living away from home for the first time; long duration before being home again
	Navigating personal boundaries/less social risk, maintaining comfort zone	Opening self to expand social sphere, greater risk-taking, more apt to step outside of comfort zone
	Find the nurse's office in the school	Find the health clinic on campus
	Small-scale day-to-day planning: college impact	Long-range planning: immediate career impact
	Employment, club activity, extracurriculars	Internship/overseas travel abroad, Work-Study
	Counseling services: school counselor, school-based supports, resource offering	Counseling services: college mental health therapists, licensed clinicians, direct services
	Money/finances: usually set, senior dues, book supplies, clothes, cafeteria account	Money/finances: tuition, room and board, fees, living expenses, travel, transportation, unsubsidized/subsidized expenses, meal plans, Greek life "rush" fees, organization fees, entertainment fees, many more "unknown" expenses
	Mode of communication: smaller scale: REMIND app, Google Classroom, Canvas, PowerSchool, Blackboard, district and high school newsletters, TV screens, ConnectEd (internal PA system overhead speaker)	Mode of communication: broad communications: Blackboard messaging, college campus alerts Email—don't check it? You'd better start now!
	Less of an urgency to "get involved" to meet people (clubs, after-school activities, sports) as peers likely know each other from middle or even elementary school	Strong urgency to get involved to meet people as everyone is *new* and *unfamiliar*
	Hard to *reinvent* oneself as many others know you	Easier to be who you want to be Fresh opportunity to reinvent yourself—no one knows the *old* you
	Self-care: others who know you may be quick to identify when you're *off* and *not yourself*, and suggest some intervention	Self-care: taking care of health as you know yourself best (and likely the only one who will key in on struggles)
	Sleep hygiene: no time to sleep in the day, schedules are more	Sleep hygiene: expect midday and midnight power naps and in

KEY TAKEAWAYS

The shift from high school to college involves more than just packing up from home and moving onto campus.

This rapid shift into adulthood forces one to navigate experiences across three significant domains: academic, social, and personal.

Many nuances from where to study and how to navigate social contexts, to learning how to navigate roommates, exercising conflict resolution skills, self-care, and establishing boundaries encompass many aspects of one's college experience.

Printed in the United States
by Baker & Taylor Publisher Services